CW00743357

PEAK
PERFORMANCE

Become More
Effective at Work

Windy Dryden
Jack Gordon

2000

Copyright © Windy Dryden and Jack Gordon 1993, 1997

All rights reserved. No part of this publication may be reproduced, stored in a retrieval system, or transmitted in any form or by any means, electronic, mechanical, photocopying, recording, or otherwise without the prior permission of the publishers.

First published in Great Britain in 1993 by Mercury Business Books Ltd
This new edition published 1997 by Management Books 2000 Ltd,
Cowcombe House,
Cowcombe Hill,
Chalford,
Gloucestershire GL6 8HP
Tel: 01285-760722. Fax: 01285-760708
e-mail: MB2000@compuserve.com

Printed and bound in Great Britain by Astron On-Line, Letchworth

This book is sold subject to the condition that it shall not, by way of trade or otherwise, be lent, resold, hired out, or otherwise circulated without the publisher's prior consent in any form of binding or cover other than that in which it is published and without a similar condition including this condition being imposed upon the subsequent purchaser.

British Library Cataloguing in Publication Data is available

ISBN 1-85252-243-7

Acknowledgement

We wish to acknowledge our indebtedness to Dr Albert Ellis. Without his seminal insights and creative work, this book could scarcely have been written.

As a self-acknowledged workaphile, we also wish to thank him for his valuable suggestions in the preparation of the final chapter of this book.

W.D. & J.G.

Training Facilities in the UK

For information on Rational-Emotive Training please contact:

The Course Organiser
Centre for Rational-Emotive Training
156 Westcombe Hill
Blackheath
London SE3 7DH

Tel: 081293 4114

To Elizabeth and Robert
Tomorrow's Peak Performers

Foreword

Most people who know me as a well-known psychologist assume that I majored in psychology in my undergraduate days. Wrong! I have a Bachelor of Business Administration degree; and without it I might well not have originated rational emotive therapy (RET) in 1955. For when I practised other kinds of therapy – particularly psychoanalysis – I found them to have some truths, but to be fully *inefficient* as therapies. So I designed RET as a more efficient kind of therapy; and so it has often proven to be over the years.

As a clinician, I was naturally interested in applying RET to many different areas, including the important aspects of life that Freud rightly categorized as 'love and work'. My first book on RET was written in 1956: How to Live With a Neurotic: At Home and at Work (Ellis, 1957). I also applied it to many different areas such as dating, sex, marriage, and family relationships, crime, and even politics.

I started to use RET, again in the 1950s, with many business and organisational people, gave talks to the students of my Alma Mater, the Baruch School of Business and Civic Administration, and was urged by my ex-professor, Dr Milton Blum, one of the world's outstanding industrial psychologists, to write a paper with him, Rational-Effectiveness Training: A New Method of Facilitating Management and Labor Relations, which was published in 1962 in *Psychological Reports*. This paper led to Dr Leonard Haber's collaborating with me, in the late 1960s, on workshops on RET for executives and managers, which we ran very successfully in New York and Miami.

My next major venture into applying RET to the workplace was my book, *Executive Leadership: The Rational-Emotive Approach*, published in 1972 and still in print. Finally, in the 1970s, the Institute for Rational Emotive Therapy in New York started its corporate services division, headed by Dr Dominic DiMattia, which has done and sponsored several researches of RET in the workplace, published a number of books and cassettes, and arranged RET workplace presentations for some of the largest corporations in the US and Europe.

Meanwhile, with and without giving due credit to RET, the management literature and training programmes have incorporated much of the main RET theory and practice, so that it is difficult to find a major book or programme that does not include considerable rational-emotive material. Much of this material is watered down and sometimes rendered almost meaningless. But workshops and training programmes by Drs DiMattia, Tom Miller, Arthur Lange, Samuel Klarrich, and Michael Bernard (to mention a few of the RET proponents), have been exceptionally popular while authoritatively presenting the RET approach.

Popular, too, I predict will be this book, *Peak Performance: Become More Effective at Work*. For no better volume, I think, now exists that clearly, incisively, and comprehensively presents the principles and practice of RET to readers who have vocational, economic, business, and work problems. Windy Dryden and Jack Gordon have worked with RET for many years, understand it thoroughly, and clarify it remarkably well. Almost everyone who works will have some of the emotional and behavioural problems they show how to deal with in this valuable self-help book. Dryden and Gordon directly, actively, and creatively teach RET, demonstrate many of its cognitive, emotive, and behavioural methods, and suggest practical, effective homework assignments.

If you have a very serious emotional problem, by all means see an (RET) psychotherapist. But if you often plague yourself with needless worries, approval needs, and low frustration tolerance that afflict most employers, managers, supervisors, employees, and workers, this book, will, if you use it, prove most helpful. Don't take my word for it. Get into this highly practical self-help manual and see for yourself.

Albert Ellis, Ph.D.,
President, Institute for Rational-Emotive Therapy
New York City

Contents

1

Fundamental Ideas

Introduction

In this chapter we aim to provide a well-tried, realistic conceptual perspective with which you can identify and tackle virtually any emotional problem that may be interfering with your functioning as an effective executive or business leader. The principles and procedures used are part of an integrated system developed by Albert Ellis, a famous clinical psychologist in New York. Known as the rational-emotive approach, it is backed by over thirty-five years of counselling work and about which a sizeable body of literature has been published (Ellis & Whiteley, 1979).

As you learn and master the A-B-Cs of Rational-Emotive Training and practise applying these principles of rational living and working to your professional and personal life, you will begin to become habituated to a practical way of thinking about yourself and your associates that will be of inestimable value to you. For Rational-Emotive Training not only offers you unusually deep insights into human relationships and suggests effective solutions to your every-day problems; it supplies you with a more appropriate outlook on life and work that may well turn out to be one of the most significant bodies of knowledge you have acquired to date and which can stand you in good stead for the rest of your life. Before we go on to explain the A-B-C Model of Emotional Disturbance, let's make clear what we mean by 'rational'.

What do we mean by 'rational'?

As used throughout this book, the term rational refers to firstly, choosing for yourself certain basic values, purposes and goals or ideals and then secondly, attempting to achieve these values or goals through the use of efficient and flexible methods while at the same time avoiding contradictory or self-defeating results. We do *not* select your values or show you what your basic goals *should* be. That is up to you. But we do assume, that in common with most people, you wish to survive and be happy. In addition, we assume that you wish to involve yourself in some line of economically remunerative business and have certain personal and organisational goals which you aim to achieve. Given these assumptions, and being aware of how easily people think, feel and behave in ways that interfere with the achievement of their goals, our aim is to show you how you can rationally, that is, efficiently, get more of what you want out of your life and less of what you don't want.

The A-B-C model

We mentioned that you have goals, desires, purposes and values. So let's begin with them. Like most people, you presumably wish to stay alive and healthy over a good number of years, to relate intimately with a few selected individuals and to achieve a reasonable degree of happiness. In addition, as an executive you also have your own agenda; you have set yourself certain personal and corporate goals. These goals might comprise becoming head of your department, or heading your organisation or getting on the board of directors. You bring these goals, consciously or unconsciously, to the daily business of living and you strive to attain certain objectives.

Now let's move to point A in the model. A stands for Activating Event, usually some unfortunate event that frustrates you or impedes you in the pursuit of your goals. As you are doubtless aware, there are probably many such hassles and roadblocks to be overcome on the way to reaching your goals – many unpleasant 'As' or Activating Events. Life could well be spelt H-A-S-S-L-E. So let's give A a realistic shape: let's make A stand for some unpleasant event or circumstance such as being criticised by your boss. That is an experience, an Activating Event, that most of us can relate to.

Next, we move to point C. C stands for your emotional Consequence or response to the Activating Event (being criticised by your boss) at A. Many people will respond to having their performance criticised by their boss by feeling depressed, or hurt, or angry.

Let's assume you are feeling depressed about the criticism. Now, your response, denoted by point C, is not caused by the unfortunate event at A, i.e. being criticised, as you might think. Your depressed mood stems from B. In the A-B-C model, B stands for your Belief System. Your Belief System comprises your beliefs, attitudes and general philosophies, the ways you habitually interpret and evaluate certain unpleasant Activating Events or Activating Experiences that happen to you. You can think of B simply as the collection of attitudes, values or philosophies that you strongly hold about the various disagreeable Activating Events or Activating Experiences in your life.

A fundamental tenet of RET, supported by an impressive amount of experimental and clinical evidence, is that your feelings or emotional reactions to these Activating Events are *largely* determined by the way you view or think about these Activating Events. In other words, and in terms of the model, *B largely causes C*. We say that B largely – rather than completely – causes C, because your feelings and moods can be influenced by drugs and certain other things that can affect your nervous system. But we claim that your feelings, especially your disturbed feelings about the various unfortunate Activating Events you experience at A, are mainly created and sustained by the way you view or think about those experiences.

It follows that if you want to stop feeling depressed, hurt or angry as the case may be, you need to examine and change the *kind* of beliefs or attitudes you hold at B about the unfortunate Activating Event you experience at A. We hope the diagram below will clarify these important points.

A = Activating Event
B = Your Beliefs about A
C = Your Emotional and Behavioural Responses to A

A does *not* cause C: **A≠ C**

B *largely* causes C: **A -------- B>>>>>>>>C**

A *contributes* (via B) to C: Without an input from A, B could not create C.

Let's put some flesh on the bare bones of the A-B-C model by giving you a 'real life' example to illustrate in a more vivid manner the points we've been trying to put across. We begin with point C in the model. C stands for how you are feeling. Let's suppose that you are feeling depressed. You are sitting at your desk feeling listless and sorry for yourself. You see the work piling up before you, but you can't bring yourself to do anything effective to deal with it. This is C. Now we look for A. What Activating or Antecedent Event(s) at point A occurred just shortly before you became self-pitying and inactive?

Let's suppose you head a large accounts department which handles the accounts and tax affairs for a number of your firm's clients. You have emerged from an interview with the Chairman of the Board who criticised your performance on a number of grounds:

- you spent too much time socialising with some of your more prestigious clients during working hours;

- a certain slackness had been recently noticed in your department;

work was being handed in late and deadlines frequently missed by a substantial margin;

- the budget you had presented for your department's activities for the coming financial year was quite unrealistic and would be severely cut back.

The Chairman didn't mince his words when he said he expected to see an immediate improvement in your performance and in the output of your department – or else!

So, here your are sitting feeling miserable and inert at C and attributing your misery to being criticised by the Chairman at A. Your friends sympathise and agree with you: 'Why, anyone would be bound to feel as badly as you do after being hauled over the coals like you were!' Right thinking? Wrong!

You have made a number of serious errors, your department has been noticeably sloppy of late, and as a result, you were criticised by the Chairman. But how could that event in the world outside cause you to feel anything deep down inside you? If external events could actually cause us to feel anything, wouldn't everybody who experienced the same activating event at A be bound to feel the same emotional consequences at C? In fact, do people respond to the same events in precisely similar ways? Obviously they don't. If the Chairman had criticised a score of department heads for their poor performance, would they all feel as inert and self-blaming as you? We think it very unlikely. Some would feel as you did, others would buckle down immediately to putting their departments in order, while one or two others might decide to tender their resignations.

'Well, if A (the activating event) is not the cause of my emotional consequence at C, what is the cause?' you ask. As we have already described the answer is B: your Belief system – the values, attitudes or philosophies which you strongly hold and with which you evaluate unpleasant events or experiences which befall you. The way in which you evaluate the various events in your life determines how you feel about them *and* how you react to them. Thinking, feeling and acting don't exist in isolation; they constantly influence each other. Alter one, and you tend to see the other two change as well. Hence the expression, 'you feel as you think.' This is an important point to keep in mind.

B stands for *Beliefs*.

Rational Beliefs (rBs) take the form of *preferences*, *likes* and *dislikes*, while *irrational* Beliefs (iBs) take the form of absolutist *demands*, *commands* and *dictates*.

In this instance, what do you suppose B consists of? First, you hold a set of rBs about what has happened to you at A:

- 'I wish I had not done poorly.'

- 'It is very unfortunate that I overdid the socialising with certain clients and allowed my department's output to go downhill.'

- 'How annoying that I failed to notice what was happening in my department and to take corrective action in time!'

- 'How frustrating that my budget was cut just when I had plans to expand!'

- 'How annoying and damaging to my prospects it is to be carpeted by the Chairman for overdoing the entertainment of certain clients, especially since he himself had originally suggested that I spend a little more time during office hours getting to know my more prestigious clients on a more personal level! I guess I interpreted his advice too generously; what a nuisance!'

How would you feel if you stuck rigorously with these rBs? If you really believed, 'I don't like being criticised by my boss', and that it's only very unfortunate, annoying and frustrating that your department did poorly and that you were personally censured for its performance, you would merely feel sorry, regretful and annoyed about these disadvantageous activating events; you would not sit for long commiserating with yourself and you would probably feel motivated to make a few changes in the way you and your department carried on your business so as to earn a better appraisement from your Board next year. Thus your emotional and behavioural responses to the activating events which preceded (but note, did not *cause*) them are *helpful* because they encourage you to do something constructive in response to these unfortunate activating events at A.

Defining rationality

Why are your rBs about the circumstances at A deemed rational? There are two criteria that make beliefs rational:

- *They are factual* – you can produce facts and data to back up such statements. There are several reasons why it was unfortunate and frustrating to be criticised, and for your department's budget to be cut back. You could show that your poor appraisement might lead to your demotion or even dismissal, or that you are unlikely to get the rise in salary you had hoped for and your plans to upgrade or expand your department would now have to be put on hold.

- *They help you to take constructive action* – rBs make you feel both determined and capable of taking action to rectify a situation. If you strongly held these rBs about being criticised by your Chairman at.A, you would naturally feel sorry and annoyed; but at the same time you would act speedily to make the situation better.

Alas! Since you are human you have a strong tendency to slip over into some highly *irrational* Beliefs. *Irrational* Beliefs (iBs) frequently involve over-generalisations and gross exaggerations, such as being convinced of something like the following:

- 'I absolutely *should not* have done poorly!'

- 'Isn't it *awful* that I was pulled up by the Chairman over my performance of my duties?'

- 'I *can't stand* failing like that!'

- 'I'm a *complete* failure for making such a hash of my job!'

- 'I'll probably *never* do well again!'

With beliefs like these you won't feel merely sorrowful and regretful, you will feel severely anxious and depressed. These are unhelpful emotional responses because they will almost certainly not motivate you to do better in future and will in all probability sap your executive ability to do anything very constructive to improve your situation.

Defining irrationality

Why are these iBs about the circumstances at A deemed irrational? Irrationality is defined by three criteria:

- *They are not factual.* Indeed, they are completely magical, essentially unconfirmable judgements or evaluations which bear no relationship to reality.

- *They are illogical.* It simply doesn't follow that because you would have preferred to have done a better job that you absolutely must have done so.

- *They lead to poor results and are self-defeating.* In other words, they don't work.

As an executive you are paid to get results and if you don't get the results you have planned for, you find out why. Then you change what needs to be changed so that you end up with the results you really do want.

In Rational-Emotive Training we aim to do precisely that. If we can show you that holding certain iBs about yourself, your associates and the world around you will almost invariably lead to poor results and block the realisation of your corporate aims and personal ambitions, wouldn't you think it worth your while to learn how to identify and eliminate these iBs? Even the most smoothly functioning machine will begin to malfunction once sand and grit get into the 'works'. In a sense, our job as Rational-Emotive Trainers is to show you how to identify and eliminate the psychological grit which impedes you from achieving the peak performance of which you are capable.

Let us provide an example of what we mean by taking each of the five iBs set out above and examining each one in turn. Our aim at this point is to convince you that these iBs simply don't make sense and therefore are untenable. To achieve that we are going to put forward an easily understandable method of quickly getting to the philosophic core of all kinds of emotional upsets and to teach you an efficient technique of uprooting them.

Point D: disputing your irrational Beliefs

The A-B-C model states that emotional upsets and the self-defeating behaviours that accompany them are not caused by events at point A, but by the iBs you hold at point B about A. The next logical step, therefore, takes us to point D. D stands for Disputing. What we do now is to challenge and dispute the validity of those iBs we previously identified by asking scientifically, factually or logically oriented questions about them. For example:

- 'Where is the evidence for this belief?'
- 'Can this assertion be proved?'
- 'What data can be produced in support of this belief?'
- 'What logical conclusion would follow if this belief were true?'

You keep probing with questions like these until you see that iBs simply don't make sense. You continue disputing them until you clearly see that they can no longer be maintained and you start to consistently give them up. It will be helpful to study the following example of the technique of disputing, using for illustration the iBs we identified and enumerated above.

An example of disputing

IB: '*I absolutely **should not** have done poorly!*'

Question: Who says you absolutely should not have done poorly? If that were true, if some law of the universe laid it down that you *should not*, absolutely should not do poorly, then how could you possibly fail to do otherwise? Obviously no such law exists. And the fact is that you did do poorly. If you failed, you failed! Therefore it makes no sense to believe that you absolutely should not have done what you certainly did do!

IB: '*Isn't it **awful** that I was pulled up by the Chairman over my performance of my duties?*'

Question: What does 'awful' mean here? It is certainly inconvenient and disadvantageous that you were criticised for your performance as you have already acknowledged. That was your *rational* belief. But doesn't 'awful' mean not merely 100 per cent inconvenient, but more than 100 per cent inconvenient? How can anything be *more* than totally painful, inconvenient or disadvantageous? How can you, or anyone else, prove that the discomfort of your being criticised for your performance is *more* than exceptionally unpleasant? Can you see that 'more' doesn't relate to anything real?

Moreover, isn't your belief that it is awful to be criticised by the Board for your poor performance imply that you *should not, must not,* be placed in this unpleasant

22

situation? We would agree that it is disadvantageous for you and a pain in the neck to be in this position, but why *shouldn't*, why *mustn't* the situation be that way? Is there some law that says you *mustn't* experience unpleasant events? If you believe that unpleasant experiences mustn't happen to you in spite of the fact that they do, aren't you demanding that the world be different from the way it actually is? As in the first example above, we have another self-contradictory hypothesis!

IB: *'I **can't stand** failing like that!'*

Question: Why *can't* you stand it? If you really couldn't stand it, you wouldn't be around any more and it would be your ghost, not you, who would be reading this book! As a human being you inevitably fail from time to time. If you were not built to withstand failure you would have perished long ago. You have to be able to withstand failure, otherwise you would be unable to survive.

     And doesn't your 'I can't stand failing' really mean that you believe you will never have any happiness again? What, *never*? What evidence could you ever produce to convince yourself that because you failed, you could never be happy again, anywhere or anytime or with any person? A very, very unlikely outcome, don't you think?

     The belief, 'I can't stand failing', when you really think about it, bears no relation to reality. You can't stand failing because you only *think* you can't.

IBs: *'I'm a **complete** failure for making such a hash of my job!'*
*'I'll probably **never** do well again!'*

Let's consider these two together:

Question: You failed on this occasion, but how does that make you a *complete* failure? Because you failed on this occasion, does that mean you must go on failing? Even if you failed again, you still wouldn't be a complete failure but only an individual who has so far been unsuccessful in achieving certain objectives. And how could you justifiably conclude that if you keep trying, you will *never* be able to do well again?

These two iBs are good examples of gross exaggeration and over-generalisation, or what we term 'all-or-nothing' thinking. When you irrationally appraise unpleasant events at point A you tend to 'awfulise' and 'catastrophise' about them and thereby create in yourself inappropriate and self-defeating emotional reactions at C. Because you see the real inconveniences, disadvantages and hassles in the world as holy horrors, your inappropriate emotional reactions do little to help you calmly accept the reality of the situation nor do they help you to vigorously act to change or improve it.

The benefits of disputing

Rational-Emotive Training, then, aims to help you replace your irrational ideas with rational philosophies of living. If you vigorously persist at point D in disputing your iBs about unpleasant activating events at point A, then you will help yourself to arrive at point E. E stands for Effects, the effects of disputing and eliminating your iBs. There are two important Effects: a cognitive (or thinking) effect (cE), and an emotional or behavioural effect (bE). A cE is a restatement of your original rational belief in a more general and stronger form. For example:

- 'There is no reason why I *should not* have done poorly because the fact is I did. What exists, exists. I am responsible for having created the conditions which lead to my poor performance and thereby incurred the criticism of the Chairman. It would have been better had I not done poorly but having done poorly in fact, it makes no sense to claim that I absolutely *should not* have done poorly.'

- 'It is *not* awful that I was hauled over the coals by the Chairman of the Board; it is only very inconvenient. Practically all poor performances of this kind in business as well as in some other areas of life are manifestly disadvantageous; but nothing is *awful*, horrible or catastrophic unless I arbitrarily define it so.'

- 'Quite obviously I can *stand* this kind of failure. I'll never *like* failing but I can gracefully lump it!'

- 'There is no evidence that I am a failure for doing badly even if I am falsely labelled one by others. I am a fallible human being for having failed but not a failure.'

- 'The fact that I did badly on that one occasion does not prove, nor ever really can, that I will never be able to do well again. In fact, the more I learn from my present and past errors, the fewer mistakes I am likely to make in future.'

An emotional or behavioural effect (bE)

You will recall that we stated that you will experience two Effects if you vigorously and continually dispute your iBs. If you change what is going on in your head at B, then you would expect to experience a changed Effect at C. As a result of acquiring a more rational set of beliefs at B, you will almost certainly feel and act in more appropriate ways when confronted by unfortunate or unpleasant activating events at point A. For example, if we assume that you have been criticised by the Board because your department turned in poor results, you will no longer feel self-pitying and depressed about your future with the company. Instead, you will feel sorry and annoyed at the setback you've experienced and determined to take corrective action to ensure that it doesn't happen again. You may decide to work harder, or to seek help in changing some of the organisation's policies which seem to you to be counter-productive, or try to get on better terms with your critics. In other words, you are more likely to succeed in changing the undesirable aspects of an obnoxious activating situation at A (such as being censured by the Board for your poor results) if you are free of emotional problems about A, than if you feel depressed and self-deprecating about your failure and subsequent censure by your Chairman.

Couldn't I just be indifferent?

You could, or you could pretend to be, but we wouldn't advise it! Here's the reason why we don't advocate adopting an attitude of indifference. First, it wouldn't be you in the sense that you would only be kidding yourself. You do care about achieving your corporate and personal goals and consequently you experience it as a setback if your performance is criticised by the upper echelons in the organisation. So why would you pretend you don't care? Isn't it because you can't bring yourself to acknowledge your failure for fear that such an admission would be too damaging to your self-esteem? If you believed that, wouldn't you be holding these iBs:

- 'I must perform outstandingly well!'

- 'If I fail to turn out an outstanding performance, as I *must*, that would be awful!'

- 'That would prove I'm no good and that I'll never be outstanding at anything I do.'

- 'I couldn't bear it if my colleagues find out!'

   By defensively claiming that you were not really bothered about the Chairman's criticism of your performance you can perhaps carry it off and even win a few sympathetic words from friendly colleagues. But like the fox in the fable of the grapes, you really do want the grapes; you do want to succeed. So how will indifference help to motivate you to act constructively and accomplish your objectives? The answer is, it won't! Apart from the fact that you are lying to yourself by pretending indifference, the more successful you are in maintaining an outwardly calm indifference, the less motivated you will feel about using your organising ability to correct your department's failures and thereby improving your chances of winning a better appraisement from the Board in future. Thus, irrational responses (including indifference) to the Board's criticism of your performance will get you nowhere, nor will they enable you to do better in future. On the other hand, rational responses will prevent you from feeling unduly upset by criticism and at the same time will motivate you to take effective action to improve your performance and take a step nearer to achieving your organisational objectives.

Not everyone aspires to become a high flyer and many employees in commerce and the civil service are quite content to adopt a laid-back attitude and achieve a just-about-average level of performance. They don't win any awards for their performance, but they don't get into serious trouble either. Such people can tick along quite happily until retirement, reserving their energy and enthusiasms for their own private concerns. While these people could theoretically benefit from Rational-Emotive Training, they are unlikely to use it.

You, however, have more ambitious objectives in mind and are more willing to devote a major part of your life and personal energy to achieving them. Very well, then. Go to it and use the rational principles we teach you in this book to help you achieve your goals with the minimum of emotional wear and tear on your nervous system. You may have thought at one time it looked 'cool' to respond to personal criticism with an attitude of indifference; but if you still think so today you will only needlessly defeat yourself.

The essential points so far

The main points we hope you have picked up so far are these:

- *You*, and not other people, create your emotional feelings and behavioural reactions at point C.

- Regardless of what others do at point A, it is not their Activating behaviour which upsets you at point C but your Beliefs about that behaviour.

- Every time you feel upset – anxious, depressed, or angry – you are probably holding both a rational and an irrational Belief.

- Your rational Belief (rB) takes the form of:

    'I don't like this at all! I wish it didn't exist, but it does. Isn't that too bad? I wish very much that I could change it!'

- Your irrational Belief (iB) takes the form of:

    'It's *awful* that this exists!'
    'I *can't stand* it!'
    'It *shouldn't* exist!'
    'I am a rotten person, or the world is a rotten place for allowing it to exist!'

- Once you recognise your iBs you can persistently challenge, question and dispute them until you succeed in minimising or eliminating them. You can often do this quite quickly and the more you work at disputing your iBs, the sooner you will succeed in ridding yourself of them.

- If you continually and vigorously dispute your iBs whenever you feel upset, you will arrive at a radically new way of looking at things. In effect you will acquire a rational, non-demanding philosophy of life which will automatically prevent you from seriously upsetting yourself about virtually anything.

- Indifference to criticism following a failure on your part to accomplish some highly desired organisational objective is really an anxiety-inspired cop-out and will do nothing to help motivate you to get back to taking specific action dedicated to achieving your objective.

'Demandingness'

The essence of emotional disturbance is demandingness, which means being needy, childlike and insisting on instant gratification, depending on the context. People find it easy, partly through biological predisposition and partly through faulty environmental upbringing, to bigotedly believe that they *need* what they want, that they *must have* whatever they wish or prefer, and that it is *awful* if other people or the world deprive them of what they think they *must have*. Irrational Beliefs take many forms.

There are innumerable expressed variations of the core iBs which lie at the root of most emotional disturbance. All of them consist, as you would now expect, of unqualified demands or dictates.

The good news is that they can all be subsumed under one or other of *three* major dictates.

Almost any emotional problem can be shown to consist of one or more of these three main iBs or dictates. Because of their importance, we have highlighted them by setting them out in the box below:

The three main irrational Beliefs

1. Because it would be highly preferable if I were outstandingly competent and/or loved, I absolutely should and must be; it's awful when I am not, and therefore I am a worthless individual.

2. Because it is highly desirable that others treat me considerately and fairly, they absolutely should and must, and they are rotten people who deserve to be utterly damned when they do not.

3. Because it is preferable that I experience pleasure rather than pain, the world absolutely should arrange this and life is horrible, and I can't bear it when the world doesn't.

These three core iBs or dictates and their derivatives lie at the root of virtually all emotional problems and self-defeating behaviours. As you proceed through this book you will be shown many illustrative examples of how these major iBs interfere with and sabotage the efficient functioning of even the most highly trained people and that unless you are shown how to recognise and uproot your own iB systems and replace them with sounder, reality-oriented philosophies, many of your most cherished personal and organisational goals are unlikely to be realised.

In view of the immense distress caused to themselves and others when people adhere strongly to any of these iBs, what rational alternatives would you suggest would make much more sense? We suggest you think about and reflect upon the three main rBs highlighted in the box below. If you learn to make these Beliefs a part and parcel of your basic philosophy so that they become automatically the way you view life's events, you stand a better chance of getting more – perhaps even much more – of what you really want out of life.

The three main rational Beliefs

1. I would strongly prefer to be outstandingly successful and/or loved and approved by certain significant others; but there's no reason why I absolutely have to be. It would be disappointing and frustrating if I fail to achieve what I want, but it would not be awful or catastrophic and I could still accept myself unconditionally and be happy.

2. I would certainly prefer others to treat me fairly and considerately but there is no reason why they absolutely should or must. If they do not treat me as I would like, that is too bad but I can stand it; and they are not rotten people but merely fallible human beings who occasionally act badly but who in no way deserve to be damned for their poor behaviour.

contd/...

The three main rational Beliefs (contd)

3. While I much prefer to experience pleasure rather than pain, there is no reason why the world must accede to my wishes. If I am unfortunate and pain or deprivation is something I may experience to a greater degree than I would wish, it is not awful, I can stand it, and I need not necessarily experience life as horrible or unbearable.

Three main Rational-Emotive Insights

To enable you to make the most of Rational-Emotive Training, it is important that you understand three basic Rational-Emotive Insights. The first of them you are already fairly familiar with.

Insight No. 1

You mainly feel the way you think. We are not saying that you are totally responsible for your emotional upsets and self-defeating behaviours. We acknowledge, as we indicated above, that you are influenced to some extent by your biology, the kind of upbringing and social learning you have been exposed to and the culture you were brought up in. None the less, you do control your emotional destiny to a degree you may not have realised. By and large you *choose* how often and intensely you upset yourself, and even how long you remain upset once you become upset. If you largely create your emotional states by the way you evaluate the various activating events in your life, it is quite on the cards that you can change your emotional states by changing the way you think.

Insight No. 2

Many people believe that events in their childhood which they perceived as traumatic at the time are the cause of emotional problems they experience as adults today. While external events such as being criticised or unloved when you were young may have contributed to your emotional traumas and subsequent behavioural reactions, they did not cause your reactions. Lacking the capacity to evaluate critically the meaning of what happened to you when you were young, you easily accepted the criticisms of parents or those in charge of you and took their criticisms as evidence that there was something wrong or lacking in you. As a consequence you may well have become emotionally disturbed over the treatment you received, or failed to receive.

Insight No. 2 is the understanding that regardless of how people disturbed themselves in the past, they are *now* disturbed because they still believe the irrational ideas with which they created their disturbance in the past and are still actively reindoctrinating themselves with these irrational and unsustainable beliefs today. If you are experiencing emotional problems today, it is not because you were 'conditioned' to hold certain iBs in the past and now do so 'automatically'. Rather, it is because you are continually reinforcing these ideas by your present unrealistic thinking and inappropriate actions or inaction.

It is useful to remember that 'conditioning' (the application of suitable rewards or punishments to obtain desired results) is really self-conditioning, as we almost always have the power of choice. This is fortunate for us, because if we perpetuate our emotional upsets and self-defeating behaviours through actively indoctrinating ourselves with irrational ideas, it follows that because we have the power to change our thinking, we can rid ourselves of our crooked ideas and unhelpful attitudes and replace them with more rational convictions and helpful attitudes.

In a nutshell, the essence of Insight No. 2 is that until you accept responsibility for the existence and continuation of your iBs and behaviours – regardless of how long ago they originated you are unlikely to make substantial inroads into changing them. Which brings us to Insight No. 3.

Insight No. 3

Insight No. 3 is the realisation and clear conviction that because many of the irrational ideas you strongly hold today have been held for quite some time and as a result have become firmly established, it follows that if you want to rid yourself of those faulty ideas and demands that are presently sustaining your troubled feelings and behaviour, there is nothing for it except hard work and practise at undermining your irrational ideas and replacing them with more realistic ideas that will lead to healthier emotions and constructive behaviour.

What comes next?

Armed with these three rational insights plus the other material in this chapter on the A-B-C model of emotional disturbance and the methods of disputing, you are now in a position to use what you have learned. In subsequent chapters you will learn by means of examples how to use your new understanding to resolve a number of common psychological problems which bedevil people today in both their working environments and private lives, and block them from achieving peak performance at work.

Summary

- *You feel as you think (Insight No. 1), and feelings and behaviour are all inter-related. External events, such as being criticised by your boss contribute to your emotional response, but they do not <u>cause</u> it.*

- *Your* disputing*feelings and behaviour in response to some activating event in your life are either appropriate and helpful, or inappropriate and self-defeating. The direction they take depends on the way you think about and evaluate whatever you perceive is happening to you. Your belief system largely determines your emotional and behavioural response to activating events.*

- *Your belief system basically consists of beliefs of two kinds: rational and irrational. Rational Beliefs are reality-based and logically demonstrable. They take the form of <u>preference</u>, <u>likes</u>, and <u>dislikes</u>.*
  Irrational Beliefs consist of unrealistic notions and unprovable assumptions or predictions, usually expressed in the form of absolutist <u>demands</u> and <u>dictates</u>.

- *Indifference to criticism of your work performance following a failure to reach your organisational target is a defence against anxiety about being thought by others to be incompetent and therefore in your own eyes worthless. Indifference inhibits you from acting incisively to correct your performance failures and de-motivates you from striving to obtain better results in future.*

- *The A-B-C model of emotional disturbance provides you with a framework for conceptualising emotional problems and identifying and separating the rational and irrational components of your belief system. Methods of challenging, questioning and disputing the iBs identified with the help of the A-B-C model help you to uproot these self-defeating beliefs and replace them with more rational convictions. These, in turn, lead to healthier feelings and more appropriate and constructive behaviours.*

• *Three major irrational ideas and their derivatives constitute the core of virtually all emotional disturbance. Because of their importance in understanding emotional disturbance and the behavioural consequences that follow from it, we identified in detail and highlighted these major irrational ideas in the text. We also provided rational alternatives to each of these beliefs.*

• *If you are currently experiencing an emotional problem, regardless of how you may have acquired it originally, you may assume that the reason it still continues to bother you is that deep down you still cling to the iB or iBs which created the problem in the first place. This is Insight No. 2.*

• *To obtain the full benefit from Rational-Emotive Training requires hard work and practise at understanding, contradicting and acting against your iBs and self-defeating habits. This is Insight No. 3.*

2

Overcoming Fear Of Failure

Have you noticed how reticent some people are to acknowledge that they have failed in some aspect of their life they consider important? It might be their marriage, their career, the upbringing of their children or their latest date with a particularly attractive member of the opposite sex. Whatever form the failure takes, it seems to be regarded as some kind of catastrophe about which the less said the better. Minor failures, or failures which are perceived as minor, are often recounted as matters of little importance, or even as occasions for hilarity: 'Boy, you should have seen my partner's face when I made a mess of that last bridge hand'; 'You should have heard the mouthful I got when I blew a tyre and arrived for dinner an hour late'.

While there may be a difference of opinion about what constitutes a 'serious failure', once someone fails to perform some activity to which the performer attaches great personal importance – be it sex with a new partner, or succeeding in winning a promotion by coming first in a job interview – there is often a marked reluctance to attribute the particular failure to some personal inadequacy or skill deficit on one's own part. Instead we find a tendency on the part of those who fail to achieve some objective, which they regard as personally important, to defensively deny they might have a problem; or if a problem is acknowledged privately, the self-deprecation for having a problem de-motivates that individual from openly acknowledging it. He or she then attributes the failure to bad luck, or lays the blame on childhood, or background or some other set of external circumstances.

We maintain, and hope to convince you, that there is nothing shameful about failing. We're not saying it doesn't matter if you fail. It can matter a great deal. This is a book about achieving peak performance, and about getting the results you want. What we are saying is that you are doing yourself no favours by defensively refusing to admit that your performance on a particular project was inadequate (for example), for fear of what others will think about you as a person when they find out.

We all fail from time to time because we are all fallible human beings. If you have a fear of failure and are loathe to acknowledge your errors, especially to your colleagues and superiors, don't upset yourself over it. We will show you presently that there is a reason why you feel like this. Then we will show you what you can do about it. But first, let's take a closer look at what we mean by 'failure'.

What is failure?

To some extent failure is partly definitional. What is seen as a tragic failure by one person may be considered to be a blessing in disguise by another. People are different – your goals and values are not necessarily the goals and values of somebody else. For example, when the communist regime in East Germany collapsed and the Berlin Wall was torn down, the communist leaders regarded the demise of their state as an unmitigated tragedy. But to millions of other Germans it was greeted with rejoicing.

When is a 'failure' not a failure?

Suppose you plan a project and after carrying out all the work exactly according to plan, you find it doesn't work. Is that a failure? If nothing can be learned from it, if nothing can be salvaged or put right and the whole thing has to be scrapped and the money put into the project cannot be recovered, then most people would agree that yes, that project was a failure. But how often can *nothing* be learned from our mistakes? Something of an inference is involved when we designate a failure as 'bad'. Suppose you design a scheme to improve the data-collection procedures for audit purposes in a group of interlocking companies. The results turn out to be no better than before you introduced your scheme. Is this a failure? Maybe. Then, subsequent investigation reveals that certain essential information from company A was not being recorded and passed on for inclusion in the group audit because of a misunderstanding on the part of certain individuals employed in that company's accounts department. Once certain changes were made your scheme worked as intended. What had appeared to be an expensive failure turned out to be a success.

Are we claiming that no one need ever be afraid of failing on some vitally important task or project? Not quite. If you were sent on a dangerous mission in which there was a distinct possibility of your being seriously injured, or even losing your life if you failed in your objective, it would be strange if you *didn't* feel fearful. Fear stimulates the release of your adrenalin to give you added strength and alertness. Fear in these circumstances is a natural life-protecting reaction. However, unless you are in a very unusual line of business, it is highly unlikely that if you fail to carry out some important assignment, your boss will recommend you for the firing squad! He may look and sound as if he'd like to, but he is scarcely likely to do so.

Even when there is general agreement that you really have failed on some project, your failure may well be unfortunate and deeply disappointing, but it is not necessarily all bad, or a total failure. In science, for example, a 'failed' experiment has often pointed the way to important discoveries which are made later. Finding out what doesn't work is often a necessary prelude to discovering what does work! In science all truths are tentative, never final or absolute. Science doesn't lay claim to absolute truths. In our opinion it is the best method we have for discovering how the world works. Since we espouse the scientific method in Rational-Emotive Training, let's turn our attention now to showing you how to use it to enable people to clearly see why they fear failure, why their fears are largely irrational or unfounded, and how they can overcome their fears and thereby become more effective at work.

The root causes of fear of failure

In Chapter 1 we introduced you to the three main irrational ideas. We said that these three ideas and their derivatives were the source of virtually all emotional upsets. In this chapter we are going to focus our attention on iB No. 1. Here it is again, highlighted in the box below:

Major irrational Belief No. 1

Because it would be highly preferable if I were outstandingly competent and/or loved, I absolutely should and must be; it's awful when I am not, and therefore I am a worthless individual.

That iB and its derivatives generate and sustain fear of failure in all its forms, including problems of shyness, feelings of inadequacy, and insecurity. However, in this chapter we will be dealing mainly with fear of failure at work. But we imagine that you will readily realise that what we have to say about fear of failing at work can, with only very minor changes, apply equally well to fear of failing in a variety of social situations. That, incidentally, is one of the bonuses of Rational-Emotive Training: solve an emotional problem in one area of your life and you will find there tends to occur a kind of ripple effect which leads to some amelioration of certain other problems in areas of your life where you may not be functioning as effectively as you would like to.

Ok, now let us focus on the main roots of fear of failure, all of which are derivatives of the first of our 'unholy trinity' of main iBs:

- 'I *must* achieve my goals because if I don't, I'm no good.'

- 'I *must* achieve my goals because if I don't, I won't win promotion and I must have what I want.'

- 'I *must not* fail to achieve my goals because if I do, other people will look down on me, and I *must have* their approval.'

These three iBs are the main roots of fear of failure. There are a few others which we'll come to presently, but for the moment let's concentrate on these three.

Irrational Belief No. 1

('I *must* achieve my goals because if I don't, I'm no good.')

First, notice that absolute 'must'. If you have followed us this far you will realise that there are no absolute 'musts', 'have-to's' or 'got-to's' in the world of human behaviour. The world of physics may be the appropriate place to talk about what must happen given certain conditions but if there were some necessity built into you that you succeed in everything you do in life, how could you possibly fail?

Do you see that when you believe 'I *must* do such-and-such', you are imposing a demand on the world that conditions be arranged that you cannot possibly fail?

Next, the notion that you have value proportional to your accomplishments, and that if you fail to accomplish some goal, you have no value at all, includes several irrational elements:

- Achievement does not match up with your intrinsic worth as a human being except by arbitrary definition. You may achieve greater happiness by achieving your goals; you can produce evidence that success brings material benefits to yourself and to the company. But feeling good about your achievements does not make you a good person, nor does feeling bad about your failures make you a 'bad' or worthless person.

• If you identify or rate your *self* according to how well you achieve your goals or perform some other activity, you deceive yourself into believing that you, as a person, possess only as much worth as that activity. Do you think that makes sense?

• If you think you 'must' achieve your goals because your self-worth depends upon it, you will be afraid to take chances, you will fear making mistakes, be anxious about failing or doing the wrong thing and avoid doing many things you might really like to try. In other words, your unrealistic aspirations together with your fragile notions of self-worth will combine to practically foredoom you to failure or to a continuing fear of failing. In what way will that help you to achieve the results you really want?

Irrational Belief No. 2

('I *must* achieve my goals because if I don't, I won't win promotion and I must have what I want.')

Once again, observe those 'musts'! We have already shown you in our comments on the example above why it is irrational and self-defeating to hold that you *must* achieve your goals, or that you *must* have anything you want. If you go over these points again you will see that there is no reason why you, or anyone else, simply *must* have something because you want it! It's fine to get what you want and it is healthy to keep trying in a determined and self-disciplined manner to succeed. But if you fail, you fail! It isn't the end of the world if you don't get that promotion this time round, it doesn't mean that you will never get promotion or that you will never be happy again. And your failure doesn't say anything about your worth as a person.

Irrational Belief No. 3

The third iB which commonly assails people with a dire fear of failure is: 'I *must not* fail to achieve my goals because if I do, other people will look down on me and I must have their approval.' The irrationalities here include:

- The demand that you *must not* fail in some endeavour is just as silly as the demand that you must succeed, and for the same reasons.

- You believe that other people will look down on you if you fail and you must have their approval. Some people won't care, but suppose that they all look down on you because you have failed. Do you have to accept their evaluation?

Obviously, you don't. Other people's views are their own responsibility. Irrespective of your achievements, some people may look up to you and think you are a great person while others may look down on you and think you are nothing. These are their thoughts. But how can these thoughts define you? Unless you believe in voodoo or some kind of magic how can their thoughts affect your attitude towards yourself?

It is fine to want other people's approval for practical reasons. If your colleagues withhold their approval of you, it often means you will not get the degree of cooperation you want from them to do an efficient job. If your boss withholds his or her approval, it might disadvantage you in material and other ways. But apart from those practical advantages why *must* you have other people's approval? Isn't it because you are telling yourself such negative statements as: 'I can accept and enjoy myself only if I do at least as well or better than other people who will then approve of me'? If you think that your worth as a human being depends on how well your performances or other aspects of yourself compare to those of other people, you will practically always feel insecure and worthless. How will that help you to function effectively and achieve your goals in life?

Three rational alternatives

What alternative rBs would you put in place of that trilogy of iBs we have just discussed? We offer you the following ideas as being much more likely to help you to achieve your executive aspirations without the tensions generated by anxiety and the dire need to excel others to attain personal 'worth':

- 'I would much prefer to achieve my goals but if I fail, that is unfortunate and frustrating. I am not a failure and I can accept myself as a fallible human who has failed on this occasion but can try to learn from my mistakes and do better in future.'

- 'I strongly prefer to achieve my goals because I might win promotion and that is something I strongly desire. If I don't get what I want, that is frustrating but not the end of the world.'

- 'I wish to succeed rather than fail because if I fail my colleagues might be less enthusiastic about giving me their cooperation and I might be disadvantaged in other ways. I would like to have other people's approval of me whether I do well or not, but if others disapprove of me, that is just too bad.'

The benefits of rational Beliefs

Once you truly make them a part of your basic system, rBs will minimise your human tendency to insist that you *must* have what you want. They will also diminish your other natural tendency to demean yourself when you fail to achieve outstandingly and to slavishly seek other people's approval before you can accept yourself as a human being with intrinsic 'worth' or value in your own right.

We will now introduce you to yet another example of irrational thinking which, if you strongly adhere to it will practically guarantee you a lifetime of woe. The emotional problems are feelings of inadequacy, fear of asserting oneself. The real problem, the problem which lies in the thinking part – the part we designate point B in the A-B-C model – is *perfectionism*.

What is perfectionism?

The essence of perfectionism can be stated thus: 'I *must* do *perfectly* well at all times. If I don't, that's terrible and I am no good. Only when I do perfectly am I worth while'.

Before we analyse the irrational thinking behind perfection in the example we give you below, we wish to make one thing clear we are definitely *not* encouraging people to lower their standards By all means strive to attain the highest standard of which you are capable, your 'peak performance'. It is healthy to be alert to ways in which you can improve your performance and to strive to reach your maximum potential. You may seldom, if ever, reach it, but by all means try! Those who achieve it report a level of pleasure and satisfaction they never forget. As Rational-Emotive trainers we endorse the pursuit of perfection in whatever field of endeavour you choose to achieve it but what we do caution against in tying your personal 'worth' to your level of accomplishment and voting yourself a place in heaven when you do well, and damning yourself to hell when you fail to achieve what you demand you *must*.

Take the case of Charlie, a fine example of perfectionism if ever we saw one. Charlie is a 33-year-old male employed in the artwork department of a large advertising agency. Charlie was good at his work and some of his artwork had been acclaimed But Charlie was unhappy. He complained of lack of self confidence, feelings of inadequacy in that he didn't feel up to the job, and what he described as a need for perfectionism.

Charlie was shown that his problems stemmed from his perfectionism. His Rational-Emotive Trainer explained it this way:

TRAINER: You're afraid of doing or saying something when you get round the table with your colleagues for a brainstorming session because you think that they will consider your suggestions stupid or something like that. So you keep your mouth shut. You're afraid that if you speak up and say something that doesn't hit the nail on the head, the others are going to think, 'Charlie hasn't a clue about what the client wants! He's no good.'

And you *are* going to agree with them – that you are no good, because you see, you are a perfectionist; you *have* to be right, every time! Everybody has to think, 'Yeah, Charlie's really on the ball!'

CHARLIE: Yes, exactly.

TRAINER: Now suppose that you weren't a perfectionist. Suppose that when it was your turn to speak you said something stupid or irrelevant and the others told you so. You could say to yourself, 'OK, I see that I may have said something stupid here but that doesn't mean that I am stupid'. If you really believed that, would you still feel inhibited about expressing your views?

CHARLIE: I suppose not. But I feel inhibited about expressing my views when I'm not sure that I'm absolutely right. Besides, I think some of the ads our client advertisers ask us to produce are a bit silly, but I don't like to say so.

TRAINER: But let's suppose that you did feel inhibited about speaking your mind. It's not just because the others might think your opinions were silly or flippant that inhibits you. It is because first, you view that as an imperfection; and second, because you're telling yourself, 'It's terrible that I have that imperfection. I should be perfect and make some comment that shows I'm really with it.' Aren't you?

CHARLIE: Well, I suppose so, yes!

TRAINER: But why should you be perfect?

CHARLIE: Because I've always thought people should live up to something, you know, to an ideal.

TRAINER: Yes, but doesn't your expression. 'living up to something' really mean two things? Doesn't it mean, firstly, setting yourself a high standard, a benchmark of quality if you like, for measuring or comparing how close some activity comes up to your benchmark, and secondly, actually carrying out that activity and trying to reach the standard you set for yourself?

CHARLIE: Yes, that's about it.

TRAINER: OK. Setting ourselves high standards to aim for in our work, our vocations, in sport and so on is fine and healthy. What's more, you can legitimately rate or measure your performances against your standards or excellence and you can keep trying to improve your performances until you reach your particular level or peak performance.

CHARLIE: Well, isn't that exactly what I *am* doing?

TRAINER: Oh yes, and if you stayed with that – of setting up your standards and then striving to reach them because that is your strong healthy *desire* – you would feel keenly disappointed if and when you failed occasionally to come up to your standards. But you would not feel depressed or worthless about it and you would not feel shy about expressing your views to your colleagues. Yet, here you are telling me you feel anxious about expressing your views in these brainstorming sessions with your colleagues, because you are afraid your remarks will indicate to those present that you haven't a clue about how the message in your client's advertisement should be presented to the target readership so as to achieve the maximum impact. Now, what are you telling yourself to create that inappropriate feeling of anxiety which inhibits you from freely expressing your views about the problem under discussion?

CHARLIE: I dunno. You tell me!

TRAINER: Well, you're convincing yourself of something like this: 'I not only want to do a perfect job by showing that I understand exactly what the client is getting al and that I know how to put the message across exactly as the client visualises it, but I absolutely *must* do so, and if I

46

fail, that would be *awful* and would prove that I'm no damn good!' Am I right?

CHARLIE: (laughing). Hey, what are you, some kind of a mind reader?

TRAINER: No, but we operate on the basis of a very good theory which enables us, once we accurately know what your feelings are, to figure out what you are telling yourself to create those feelings. There's no magic about it. We don't believe in magic. So, now that you understand how you make and keep yourself anxious, what had you better do to rid yourself of these self-defeating feelings and give your natural ability the chance to show what you can do?

CHARLIE: I guess I'd better change my ideas a bit so that I don't see my personal worth as being dependent on whether I do well or not.

TRAINER: Right. As soon as you tie your personal worth, your value to yourself as a human being, to achieving some arbitrary definition or standard of perfection, you're in trouble. For even if you succeed in doing the perfect job this time round, you're still going to feel anxious about doing poorly the next time, because you're demanding, 'I must not fail, I must not fail!' Then when you do fail to produce the kind of masterpiece that you demand of yourself you must produce, you flagellate yourself unmercifully for your 'deficiency' and feel miserable. Heads or tails, you suffer!

CHARLIE: Yes, I see that now.

TRAINER: Yes, and even without your perfectionism, it seems from what your colleagues tell me, that in your line of work, it seldom happens that your people come up with just the right proposals the first time round, and the client is satisfied. Even your best efforts are sent back for reconsideration because the client thinks they are too this or too that, or they lack impact, or they fail to get the client's message across in just the way he or she visualises it. So on purely practical grounds why give yourself a hard time because you fail to come up at your first attempt with a piece of artwork which the client will think is the best thing to come out since the painting of the Crucifixion?

CHARLIE: Yeah, it does seem silly since, as you say, we hardly ever make it at the first attempt and sometimes not even after the third or fourth. But how do I overcome my perfectionism? That's the real issue, isn't it?

The irrational demand for perfection lies behind being unduly fearful of saying the 'wrong' thing or not looking as you 'should', or in short, feeling shy or inhibited as Charlie was about speaking up in the discussion group. The important point to grasp here is that the reason why you are unduly fearful about doing or saying the 'wrong' thing is that other people might criticise or not like you for it, and you then foolishly rate yourself as no good. You have this idea that others must accept you and view you in a favourable light at all times. It is this demand for esteem on the part of others which, by arbitrary definition you think you must have before you can accept yourself, which leads to your 'self-downing'. In effect, you are saying, 'If I have a trait which I and/or other people consider unacceptable, I am, therefore, no good, a non-person.'

Challenge and dispute your perfectionist Beliefs! Ask yourself questions such as: 'Why does a deficiency or failure make me less of a person?'; or 'If I have a deficiency of some kind, does that make me a deficient person?' If you look for evidence for the belief that having a deficiency or defect makes you a deficient or defective person, you won't find any!

The key lesson here is that *you* do not equal your traits, your actions or your various behaviours. Over the course of your lifetime you will perform many actions and exhibit many traits OR characteristics, some of which you and/or others will rate highly, some not so highly and some you will feel neutral about. How could you ever arrive at an overall assessment of yourself as a person based upon a global evaluation of the totality of your traits and characteristics? Remember, too, that your characteristics are not static but ever changing over the period of your life.

Understanding that you cannot rate a person, is the key to reducing perfectionism and the anxiety and self-denigration that stem from it.

The so-called fear of success

You may be wondering how on earth fear of success fits in with fear of failure. Aren't these two things diametrically opposite, you may well ask? The answer is no, not really. Of course, success is indeed the opposite of failure, but we are not talking of success as such but of success with a fear of subsequent failure attached to it. That is why we term it the 'so-called fear of success'. *The so-called fear of success is fear of failing later.*

If you fear success it is because deep down you feel you are no good. If you succeed, you succeed in spite of your habit of self-downing or negativity. You feel you are an impostor, that the whole thing was just a fluke and that sooner or later people will find you out and discover what a fraud you are. Rather than face that 'horror' you avoid competing and thereby avoid being shown up for the inadequate person you think you are.

The antidote to this form of fear, as was shown in the previous examples, is to vigorously challenge the ideas that:

- I must appear perfect in my own eyes as well as in the eyes of those who are associated with me.

- It's awful if I don't do so.

- If I have flaws, that makes me a rotten person.

Question these Beliefs by looking for evidence to support them. If you persist at doing so you will come to see how irrational and unhelpful they are.

You can reinforce your questioning by pushing yourself to do whatever it is that you are fearful of doing- such as going in for competitions, speaking up at public meetings, or going for job interviews.

Gradually you will learn to accept yourself with your imperfections. We all have some! If other people disapprove of your performance or behaviour, don't take them too seriously. Objectively decide whether they have a point and, if they do, act to change whatever you think would better be changed.

But remember, negatively rating your *self*, your totality, on the basis of having some negative traits is the reason why you fear criticism or failure and demand perfection. Being over afraid of other people's opinions and making yourself anxious and afraid to assert yourself is not going to help you achieve success in your business or find happiness in your personal life.

The rational alternative to perfectionism

If you have understood us so far and concluded that the ideas underlining perfectionism are untenable and can lead only to emotional misery, you will want to know why adopting rational alternative ideas will lead to better performance than perfectionism. We would put it this way: when you realise and accept that your personal worth is not the issue – that you are not putting yourself on the line, as it were, every time you set out to achieve a highly valued goal – the pressure on you to achieve at all costs will be off. You are still highly motivated but now you are free to marshal your brains and talent and harness your energy and resources to attaining your objective without the nagging fear that your personal worth is at stake.

You can rationally believe the following: 'I can strive to attain the highest standards in my work or vocational pursuits of which I am capable but there is no all-or-nothing necessity that I do so. If my accomplishments sometimes do not reach the highest standards I aim to achieve, that is unfortunate but hardly catastrophic and I am not a total failure but merely a fallible human who occasionally fails and who can learn from these experiences to do better in future.'

Put another way, you can strive to do *your* best rather than obsess yourself with being *the* best. You are not out to prove how superior you are to others and thereby falsely esteem yourself a better *person*.

You can honestly strive to win mastery over your material in your chosen field of expertise, be it in business or sport or whatever. But you would be wise to aim to become a better *performer* or a better *achiever* than others, rather than try to prove yourself a better *person*.

Won't giving up perfectionism lead to mediocrity? This is a question we are sometimes asked. The answer is Not necessarily. If you want to produce a near-perfect work, to turn out a virtually flawless performance of some kind, that is fine. We are all for the pursuit of excellence in what you *do* or in what you *make*. But neither *you* nor anyone else will ever exist as perfect beings. We humans remain as essentially fallible beings. If your drive to excel others is motivated by the desire to become King or Queen of the May, to 'prove' to yourself and others how much of a 'better' person you are, you will be constantly living on the edge of anxiety and hostility and *less* likely to achieve the level of performance you are theoretically capable of. Moreover, life is essentially uncertain; seldom will perfect solutions to problems and difficulties emerge as a result of even your best efforts, and consequently you may find that compromises represent the best reasonable or practicable solutions. If you are hell bent on always getting the perfect answer to your problems, you will tend to overlook better, more *feasible* solutions, and wind up with poor and ineffective ones.

Strive for excellence, then, in what you do, because of the material and other benefits that flow from excellence, not because of the greater self-esteem you falsely believe you acquire as a result of achieving excellence.

Self-management techniques

Once you accept that your performance is that which can legitimately be rated, but that your performance says nothing about you as a person, you can take a number of steps to improve it. You presumably wish to go far in your field, perhaps to reach the top. In that case there are a few things to bear in mind in addition to those specialised courses in higher management in which you will doubtless be interested.

Learn from peak performers

How do they manage their day? They have only 24 hours like everybody else, so how come they seem to get through twice as much work as those around them and still achieve such impressive results? Study what they do and what they don't do!

Set yourself realistic goals

Set yourself something to shoot for, something you can reasonably hope to achieve within a realistic time frame. If you slip up, don't waste your precious time by blaming yourself for your lapse. Look instead at what you did or failed to do. Did you unwisely spend too much time in socialising during work hours with your colleagues? Perhaps you devoted too much time to turning out a perfect performance of some relatively unimportant but pleasantly interesting task? Try to focus on the most important things to be done by you and your subordinates *now*. Then act accordingly.

Experiment with different ways of approaching tasks

Does there seem a need for new ideas, new ways of tackling the tasks before you? How about trying a brainstorming approach? Maybe someone in your staff or a colleague has a bright idea worth trying. Check on routines that have become formally established. Are they still really necessary? We can become comfortable with routine, sometimes too comfortable for our own good. These routines may have been useful, money-saving devices at one time, but can they still be justified?

Welcome appraisal of your performance

If your performance is criticised, listen and take note. Your personal 'worth' isn't at stake! Not all criticisms of your performance are necessarily accurate but some of them probably are! If you have over-come your need for perfectionism you should be able to take criticism without feeling like some kind of an idiot. If you have failed in some important respect, that is too bad, but it doesn't make you a failure and it isn't the end of the world.

Don't be afraid to ask for feedback if it has not been offered, but you think it would be useful. The person who is doing your appraisal may be waiting to see how interested you are in finding out how you can improve your overall performance.

Give yourself credit

You can give yourself a pat on the back for what you know you have done well. If you still have some way to go before you reach the stan-dard you believe you are capable of achieving, give yourself credit for what you have achieved, then figure out what you can do to improve your performance. Think of it as a gap to be closed; you are already halfway there!

Confidence comes with doing

Sometimes people will tell us: 'I have to feel confident before I start this'; or 'I need to feel comfortable about doing that sort of thing.' We use the term 'confidence' to mean work-confidence or achievement-confidence. Work-confidence exists when you can tell yourself: 'I have succeeded at this task in the past and I am confident I can do so again.' Until you have actually done something you cannot lay claim to being confident you can do it again. Note that work-confidence cannot give you *self*-confidence. We prefer not to use the term 'self-confidence' because it implies a form of self-rating. Self-acceptance is better. It is unconditional. You can accept yourself regardless of whether you do well or win other people's approval. Even the term self-acceptance leaves something to be desired since one's 'self' or 'ego' cannot be accurately defined. However, if you keep in mind the distinction we made between rating your traits or behaviour and rating your 'self', you can avoid falling into the self-rating trap.

If you want to feel comfortable or confident about carrying out some task or activity, there is nothing for it but to figure out how best you can go about it, and then go ahead and do it. If you do not do too well the first time, find out what you did incorrectly or inadequately and use that experience to improve your performance the next time. The more you practise doing something reasonably well, the sooner you will feel confident and comfortable about doing that activity in future.

Life is for living

Everyone has his or her limitations, but that need not mean you cannot live your life to your fullest potential. In this chapter we have shown you how anxiety inhibits you from achieving your full potential as a business executive and as a human being. If you conscientiously strive to master the principles of rational-emotive thinking that we have set out in this book, you can live a minimally anxious life and refuse to make yourself upset over virtually *anything*. If you choose to make the purpose of your existence the *enjoyment* of both your present and future, rather than seek just the 'pride' of outstanding achievement, you are more likely to reach peak performance and both enjoy and achieve success in the process of attaining your corporate and personal goals.

Summary

- *We discussed what failure means and argued that not all failures are hopelessly bad or irretrievable.*

- *We dealt with the root causes of fear of failure and showed that these root causes were derivatives of main iB No. 1: 'Because it would be highly preferable if I were outstandingly competent and/or loved, I absolutely should and must be; it's awful when I am not, and therefore I am a worthless individual.'*

- *We discussed each of these three irrational ideas and showed how they created and maintained a fear of failure.*

- *Three rational alternatives were then suggested to replace the three ideas which were identified as the root causes of fear of failure.*

- *We then dealt at length with the problem of perfectionism and showed by means of an example how this self-defeating notion arose from falsely identifying one's personal 'worth' as a human with one's traits and behaviour. We also showed how various other emotional and behavioural problems stemmed from the pernicious concept, 'I must be perfect'.*

- *We also showed that the so-called fear of success was really a fear of failure in disguise.*

- *After presenting you with a rational alternative to perfectionism, we described a number of self-management techniques you could employ to improve your performance and ended with some advice on reaching your level of peak performance.*

3

Become A Healthy And Creative Risk-Taker

The evaluation of risk

In this section we will not be discussing the techniques for evaluating risk. While it is sane and sensible to weigh the pros and cons of taking decisions involving a considerable degree of risk, risk evaluation is a specialised area in the organisational world. It covers investment decision-making, insurance, marketing a new product, etc. We are assuming that either you have already acquired the relevant expertise in your particular line of business, or at least you know where you can find it.

Our purpose is twofold: firstly, to uncover the emotional blocks and self-sabotaging beliefs which impede rational and effective decision-making where a considerable element of risk is involved; and secondly, to show how the acquisition of rational beliefs and attitudes can encourage healthy risk-taking and stimulate creativity with the goal of enabling you to achieve your peak level of performance.

The inevitability of risk

Life is a constant process of change. Our environment is changing and we ourselves are changing. Our bodies change, our ideas, goals and values change. We only stop changing when the ongoing biological processes inside us which sustain our life finally come to a halt. We are swept along on a river of change and at no time since the dawn of human history has the pace of change been so rapid as it is now. We confront and accommodate changes today which would have seemed inconceivable in our grandparents' time. And the pace of change, as social thinkers and futurologists such as Alvin Toffler have pointed out, is accelerating.

However, not all change lies outside our control. Indeed, the more we are subjected to change, the more opportunities we are presented with to initiate change, to modify our environment or our life-styles more to our liking. For example, the pace of technological change throughout the twentieth century has ushered in new life-styles, ways of living and working which were quite outside the experience of earlier generations. At the same time, the emergence of these new life-styles has opened up even more possibilities and permutations for change with their accompanying pressures on us to choose and to make decisions. Whenever we choose to take option A rather than option B, or C, etc., we *take a risk*. Even by choosing *not* to change those things that are within our power to change, we take a risk. Even inaction carries its own risks.

The meaning of risk

First of all, we can seldom, if ever, predict accurately the outcome of our choices and decisions; every time we take a risk we are exposing ourselves to the unknown. By intelligently assessing the degree of risk we may achieve the desired outcome, but there is no guarantee that we will. Secondly, risk is more accurately perceived as a process, rather than an outcome. It may be tempting to imagine that by taking certain risks which we estimate have a high probability of turning out as we desire, we will get things 'just right', and that no further changes will be made and we can sit back and enjoy what we have accomplished.

Well, good luck! Even if you get things under control, life will see to it that your status quo is short-lived. Life is neither Utopia nor misery because life isn't static. We cannot halt the flow of change. Change is the only continuity you will ever experience so long as you are alive. But the great plus point is that change brings with it the continuing opportunity to modify and shape change. And through accepting that we are both the products and agents of change in an uncertain world, we are offered the possibility of achieving real personal growth.

Types of risk

In this book we shall not be discussing the kind of personal and inter-personal risks which mainly occur in our private life. Whether to risk marriage, or divorce, to start a family, to pack in a good job and start again in something new, to go into or come out of retirement, to emigrate – these are typical of the risks we might consider taking, or not taking. There are several good books which deal adequately with this fascinating area of life. Two eminently readable discussions of personal risk which we can recommend are by Siegelman and Viscott (see References). Let's turn our attention now to identifying the more significant components of healthy risk-taking.

What is a healthy risk?

When you take a risk, you seek out new, unknown and potentially dangerous situations. We are not concerned here with outcomes which may be dangerous in the physical sense, such as venturing on a new ski run down a mountain side you know relatively little about. We are thinking more of ventures which, if they failed, could bankrupt your company or lose you your job. These failures and misfortunes could come about through irrational decision-making in one of two ways:

firstly, they could be brought on by failure to take decisive action at a critical moment indecision; and secondly, they could be precipitated by impulsiveness, by acting too quickly or before the pros and cons had been properly weighed and evaluated. In a moment we shall return to examine both these forms of irrational decision-making and identify the underlying iBs which lead to them.

As a decision-maker you accept that nothing is certain; none of your decisions carry a guarantee of success. You value flexibility. You try to steer a middle course between being under-decisive and over-decisive.

Taking a healthy risk means that you are about to take an important decision which, if it works out as you hope and believe it will, is likely to entail certain changes which will have important and desired consequences both for your organisation and for you personally. You have carefully assessed the chances of a successful outcome to your proposed action, and you have also given equally careful consideration to the downside potential – to the real possibility of failure and what *that* would mean for your organisation and for you personally. The final answer is that you estimate the chance of success as, say, 75 per cent or better. Assuming that 75 per cent meets your Board's criterion, the level at which they will authorise you to launch your multi-million pound project, what do you do then? You ACT! That's what you do. No shilly-shallying, no saying to yourself, 'maybe I should wait!' You go ahead and do it. You've done your best, you have checked and re-checked the figures and each time you have come up with the same answer: it's worth taking the risk and going ahead. You still rationally accept the possibility of error and the even greater possibility that the whole thing could crash for reasons that probably would have nothing to do with you reasons lying far beyond your control. But you know that life itself is a risk, that you live and work in a competitive world, and that there is an even greater risk of your company eventually going out of business if you just sit tight and do nothing. In life, nobody is excused from making choices, and we have to live with the consequences.

Irrational decision-making: the fundamental causes

Now let's take a closer look at what can prevent you from taking a healthy risk. You will recall we drew your attention to two forms of irrational decision-making: indecision was one, impulsiveness was the other.

Indecision

Let's assume in line with what we have been discussing under the heading of healthy risk-taking, that it has fallen to you to take a decision involving a considerable risk to the continued existence of your company. You have voted to spend a huge sum of money to carry out your decision, the entire workforce will be affected by the outcome and the future growth and development of your company is at stake.

Your analysis of the risk involved leads to the conclusion that it is worth taking the chance: 'We go ahead.' But you put off giving the word to go ahead. You feel more and more anxious as the final deadline for action draws near. You postpone taking action because *not* acting relieves the anxiety in the short term but is a poor solution in the longer term. Relieving your anxiety temporarily by postponing the action that you know will almost certainly be called for shortly may lead to even greater anxiety later.

In A-B-C terms, we can say that point A represents your decision to take an action which will have repercussions for your entire company. Point C stands for your feeling of growing anxiety and your increasing reluctance to act. Now, there are two kinds of anxiety, and one or both of them could be present in this case.

Take the first one which we will call *discomfort anxiety*. This stems from a *demand* for certainty that life be predictable and without too many hassles. Does that demand remind you of major *iB No. 3* which we introduced you to in the first chapter? We hope so – it conveys the same underlying idea! Here it is again, highlighted in the box:

Major irrational Belief No. 3

Because it is preferable that I experience pleasure rather than pain, the world absolutely should arrange this and life is horrible, and I can't bear it when the world doesn't.

These major iBs have many derivatives. What do you think you would be telling yourself in the situation described above to bring on this feeling of acute anxiety? Probably you would be telling yourself something like:

- 'I *must* feel certain that this decision of mine is right!'

- 'It's *awful* not knowing what the outcome will be, and I *can't stand* this uncomfortable feeling of uncertainty!'

Now study these rational alternative beliefs:

- 'I'd like to be certain that this decision of mine is right, but I don't need such certainty. Since I don't control the world there is no way that I can be certain of the outcome of any decisions I may take.'

- 'It is not awful but rather a matter of some concern to me that the outcome of my decisions cannot be predicted with certainty. Nevertheless, that's the way it is; there is no certainty.'

- 'It isn't unbearable that uncertainty exists in the world, and there is no reason why it shouldn't exist. What exists, exists. I may not like it but I can definitely stand it.'

To summarise where we are at this point: irrational Belief No. 3 and its derivatives generate *discomfort anxiety*. Rational beliefs promote realistic assessment of the situation and lead to appropriate concern about the outcome.

Ego anxiety

The other form anxiety takes we shall call ego anxiety, and it can be just as disruptive of your ability to act decisively. Like its twin, discomfort anxiety, the irrational ideas which generate ego anxiety are derivatives of another major irrational belief – in this case major irrational Belief No. 1. Once again we highlight it for you:

Major irrational Belief No. 1

Because it would be highly preferable if I were outstandingly competent and/or loved, I absolutely should and must be; it's awful when I am not, and therefore I am a worthless individual.

A derivative of this highly irrational belief which typically gives rise to ego anxiety in the situation we are discussing is:

- 'I must perform well and win the approval of important people in the organisation. If I fail to do well and win approval I am an inadequate person.'

Now consider these rational alternative beliefs:

- 'I prefer to do well and win the approval of significant people but there is no reason why I absolutely *must* do so.'

- 'There are practical advantages to acting competently, making sound decisions, acting decisively and winning others' approval. But if at times my decisions turn out badly that is unfortunate but I can still accept myself in spite of my failures and learn from my mistakes to do better in future.'

To summarise what we know so far: irrational Belief No. 1 and its derivatives generate *ego anxiety*. Rational beliefs promote: self-acceptance, flexible thinking, and motivation.

In practical situations such as the one we are discussing, the irrational Beliefs which you will encounter are almost always derivatives of one or more of the three major irrational Beliefs you met in Chapter 1. You will find it useful to go back occasionally to Chapter 1 and check this out. It will help you to get your bearings when you try to put a problem you are experiencing into the A-B-C framework, and it will facilitate your choice of the appropriate disputing strategy. Remember, your aim throughout is to identify and ferret out those self-defeating beliefs and ideas which mar your efforts to reach peak performance and to replace them with rational, helpful alternatives. Our aim is to provide you with the appropriate tools and the knowledge of how to use them to achieve your aim.

So, getting back to the problem of indecision, what are we looking for? Why are you avoiding implementing tough decisions? That's the bottom line, isn't it? That is the behavioural consequence, the reaction to your anxiety which, in turn, is created by your irrational absolutist thinking. Well, we have now identified certain irrational beliefs and the equally irrational conclusions such as:

- 'It's awful that I don't know for certain what the outcome of my decision will be, and I can't stand the discomfort of not knowing.' *(Discomfort anxiety)*

And we have the equally irrational:

- 'If I took the decision and it didn't work out, I'd be no good.' *(Ego anxiety)*

The first of these two iBs goes with the philosophy that life must be easy and comfortable and that it would be awful if it were not. The second paraphrases the perfectionist notion that one must be 100 per cent competent and successful at all times and if not, then one is worthless. Why does a thinking, reasonable person like you come to hold these ideas?

Where's my guarantee?

It is not because you want to know how your decision is going to turn out. If you simply desired to know the outcome, and stayed with just the desire, even a strong desire, you would feel appropriately concerned but not paralysed by panic into inaction. Accepting that nothing is certain, that life is governed by probabilities, you would act on your decision and perhaps arrange for some fallback strategy to come into operation should your original decision turn out to have been wrong.

But you are dithering and worrying because you are demanding a guarantee that things will work out well for you before you take action. That's the only thing that would satisfy you with your philosophy: a *guarantee* that your decision must prove the right one. How are you going to get that? How are you going to get a guarantee that *any* decisions you make will always be right? If you ever find such a guarantee, please let us know; we will pay you handsomely for it! Actually, we can give you the *RET Guarantee* and it's given free: 'I guarantee that you will stay indecisive and uncreative as long as you demand a guarantee!'

The rational alternative

What is the rational alternative to demanding a guarantee? If indecision is your problem, the way to overcome it is to truly believe and accept that you *don't need* certainty. Suppose you strongly convinced yourself: 'I very much want my plan to succeed, but there is no law of the universe which says it *has* to. I don't *need* to know that my decision will prove to be the correct one, though I truly desire and hope that it will be. But if I'm proved wrong, that will be very disappointing and I will feel very sorry. But I will get over the disappointment and maybe learn something useful from the experience, not least that when the chips are down I have the courage of my convictions and can act decisively when called upon.'

If you convinced yourself of that, you would feel concerned about the outcome of implementing your decision and determined to over-look nothing which might influence the final outcome. But once your decision was made you would act responsibly to implement it and await the outcome with healthy concern.

We can now summarise what we have learned about indecision in the following two tables.

Irrational Beliefs	Emotional and behavioural consequences
1. 'I *must* be certain my decision is right!'	
2. 'It's *awful* not knowing how my decisions will turn out!'	*Discomfort anxiety*
3. 'I *can't stand* this feeling of uncertainty!'	
4. 'I *must* perform well and win the approval of important people in the organisation.'	*Indecision*
5. 'If I fail to do well and win approval I am an inadequate person.'	*Ego anxiety*

Table 1

Now study Table 2 which summarises the rational alternative Beliefs you could hold about the same situation. You will find it help-ful to compare the two tables. Tables 1 and 2 enable you to compare directly the effects on your emotional state and subsequent behaviour of holding irrational versus rational Beliefs.

Rational Beliefs	Emotional and behavioural consequences
1. 'I'd like to be certain that this decision of mine is right, but I don't need such certainty. Since I don't control the world there is no way I can be certain of the outcome of any decisions I may take.'	*Ability to act decisively*
2. 'It is not awful but a matter of some concern to me that the outcome of my decisions cannot be predicted with certainty. Nevertheless, that's the way it is; there is no certainty.'	*Can await outcome with adequate concern*
3. 'It isn't unbearable that uncertainty exists in the world, and there is no reason why it shouldn't exist. What exists, exists. I may not like it but I can definitely stand it.'	*Can tolerate uncertainty*
4. 'I prefer to do well and win the approval of important people in the organisation but there is no reason why I absolutely must do so.'	*Self acceptance*
5. 'If at times I fail to do well and win approval that only proves that I am a fallible human being. I can still accept myself in spite of my failures and learn from my mistakes to do better in future.'	*Flexible thinking motivating*

Table 2

Impulsiveness

This, too, can be a problem! The executive who is impulsive makes choices – the trouble is he or she tends to oversimplify things and makes decisions too quickly and rashly. On the face of it there are some apparent advantages to this kind of decision-making. It saves time, it is usually clear and precise, it lets other members of the organisation know where they stand, subordinates particularly appreciate it, and sometimes it works surprisingly well. But think of the risk, especially if the future existence of the organisation may be at stake!

When you act over-decisively or impulsively you tend to hold the two main iBs we highlighted in Chapter 1 and which we discussed above in our treatment of indecision. Assume that point A stands for the same situation we discussed when dealing with indecision. At A you made a decision, and at point C you rashly take the specified action – to the surprise of the Board who invite you to explain your behaviour.

At point B you hold a fairly rational Belief – the belief you try to convince the Board motivated you to act so decisively: 'I think it important not to miss the boat. My analysis convinced me, as it did you gentlemen when you agreed and authorised the expenditure, that time is of the essence. We can't afford to be seen dragging our feet over this project or we could lose out entirely.' When the Chairman asked you were you not a little bit hasty in putting the plan into operation and had you fully evaluated the downside potential of your project, you replied: 'Well, maybe I was a little bit quick off the mark, but I don't know. If we delayed acting on this, we could end up with nothing.'

But your iBs were really the driving force behind your decision. The first one was probably a derivative of major iB No. 1: 'I must perform well and win the approval of important people in the organisation. If I fail to do well and win approval I am an inadequate person.'

In the context of your situation you probably were telling yourself a derivative that went something like: 'Boy, what a chance this is to prove what a really outstanding decision-maker I really am! I simply *must* succeed with this one and if I don't that will be awful; it would prove I'm no good and I couldn't stand that!'

With beliefs like that you would feel anxious about the possibility of not getting what you are demanding you must get, and you quite probably would feel hostile towards anyone whom you thought might be blocking you. But you make things still worse for yourself by believing a derivative of major iB No.3: 'I don't see why I have to look at every single thing that could go wrong! Dammit, I'm not going to be put off by all this nitpicking. Why should I go through all this hassle, checking and re-checking the calculations! I *can't stand* all this waiting! Life shouldn't be so difficult! I'll be the laughing stock of the whole firm if this thing doesn't come off, and I'll never be happy again. To hell with it! "He who hesitates is lost!" '

When these highly irrational notions control your thinking, you can hardly feel anything else but anxious about the possibility of failure and dismissive of those who counsel caution. Also, having staked your personal worth on achieving a successful outcome, then if your enterprise fails, the experience will have been dearly bought. *What is the rational alternative?* If being impulsive is a problem for you, the way to rid yourself of it is to challenge and dispute the two iBs which we identified as the cause of it. Thus, you would take irrational Belief No. 1 and debate it as follows:

Question: Why *must* I perform well and win the approval of significant people in the organisation?

Answer: There is no 'must' about it. I would certainly like to do well and win approval from those important people who matter to me, but I don't have to. There is no law of the universe stating that I *must* perform well. If there were such a law, how could I avoid performing well all the time? Obviously no such law exists except the law that I make up in my own head!

Question: In what way am I an inadequate person if I fail to do well and win approval?

Answer: Although my deeds, acts and performances can be rated, how can *I* be given any global rating, measurement or score? I am an ever-changing process and too complex to be given a single rating that would be meaningful. I cannot legitimately rate myself as an inadequate person because one of my acts – impulsively making a wrong decision and implementing it- was below the standard expected of me.

Now let us examine the derivation of irrational Belief No. 3, (see page 61).

Question: If going back through all those tedious calculations is an inconvenience, why shouldn't you be somewhat inconvenienced? And why shouldn't life be difficult at times? Is there a law of the universe which says that life must be easy and that we must get what we want quickly and without too much inconvenience?

Answer: Obviously there is no such law. For if such a law did exist, we would always get what we desired, pronto, and without having to try very hard. Since no such law exists, there is therefore no sense in demanding that something that does not exist *must* exist.

   Clearly, it would be in your own – and your organisation's – best interests to unrebelliously perform all necessary calculations to reduce the uncertainty factor in your decision to as low a value as possible.

Question: Where is the evidence that you 'can't stand all this waiting'?

Answer: If you think about it, you can stand anything until you are dead! Will patiently waiting for those calculations of the risk involved to be vindicated by painstaking checks cause you to expire? Hardly likely!

Question: If you have done everything you could reasonably be expected to do, but the operation still fails, is it likely that you would become the laughing stock of the entire organisation and never know happiness again?

Answer: If your plan were to fail, a few of your detractors might foolishly laugh, but the majority would be too concerned about their future to consider failure a laughing matter. Success and failure are part and parcel of life and one failure does not make you a hopeless person who can never know happiness again.

Acquiring a new outlook

If you vigorously persist at disputing your iBs you will arrive at a more rational way of looking at your problem. You will come to hold a more rational Belief about your decision-making style.

Thus, you will become convinced that:

- 'I prefer to do well and win approval for my decisions, because there are practical advantages in doing do. But I don't *have to* do well or win anyone's approval.'

- 'There is not, nor ever can be, any evidence that I am an inadequate person for doing poorly. Nor can the fact that I performed poorly on one occasion ever prove that I can never do well in the future. The more I learn from my past and present errors the fewer I am likely to make later on.

Once you overcome the irrational idea that life must be predictable and without too many problems and hassles you will tend to acquire more rBs about your situation. Thus you could rationally believe:

- 'It's a pain that life throws up so many problems and we have to forgo doing many other things that would bring us more pleasure. Tough, but that's how it is! Now let me see what I can do to solve or minimise these problems so that we have fewer of them in the future. If I succeed, fine. But if I don't, it isn't terrible and I can live happily in spite of, or even because of problems, for we humans are basically problem-solving animals.'

Your feelings will be different

As you would now expect, changing the way you think changes the way you feel. Instead of feeling anxious about the possibility of making a poor decision, you will now tend to feel appropriately concerned about the possibility of things going wrong, and you will tend to be more attentive to the views of others and less hell bent on going it alone.

You will tend to act differently

As your feelings change in response to your new rBs, so too will your behaviour. You will become more motivated to examine your decision-making style, to ask yourself and honestly answer questions such as: 'Am I too impulsive? Do I act prematurely and thereby take foolhardy risks?'; or, 'Am I indecisive, do I unnecessarily postpone implementing decisions once I have convinced myself that these decisions are the ones that best fit the facts at my disposal?' You will risk asking your colleagues for their honest opinions and be ready to listen objectively to their views and criticisms without putting yourself down. That is yet another benefit arising from a more rational philosophy.

What if you fail?

So far, we've been discussing the iBs which lie behind two decision-making styles which tend to frustrate your ability to take healthy risks. We mentioned the possibility of your decisions turning out to be mistaken but we did not go into the question of how you would feel if your decisions actually were mistaken. Let us look at that now.

How would you feel if your decisions led to your company's demise? The answer is, it depends on how you evaluate that misfortune. We are not talking now about decision-making style. That is not the issue. The issue now is how do you feel about having been the instigator of a course of action which *apparently* led to your firm's liquidation? We emphasise the word 'apparently' because it need not necessarily have been your fault that things went badly wrong. As we stated earlier, when you take a major risk, things can go wrong for reasons quite unconnected with you or your decisions or lack of them. The world is a complicated place and nobody controls it. Anything can happen, and nobody can predict what will happen. However, let's suppose that there is no doubt about it: your decision was seriously mistaken and the consequence was that your organisation went bust.

In answer to our question, most people would answer: 'I would feel ashamed if I made a decision like that!' Why? To see why, return to the page where we set out iB No. 1. Here it is again:

Major irrational Belief No. 1

'I must perform well and win the approval of important people in the organisation. If I fail to do well and win approval I am an *inadequate person.*'

Now, since you failed to perform well as you demanded you *must*, you 'logically' concluded that you are an inadequate person. Furthermore, you know that your failure cannot be kept secret. It may not become common knowledge, but at least your friends and acquaintances in the business world will get to hear about the demise of your company and of your alleged part in bringing it about. Because you know that they will know, you also infer: 'Once my friends and others I know in the business world see that I am no good, they will remember it, and I'll never be able to face them again.'

If you believed the iB and the inference drawn from it, you would feel ashamed, because shame is what one feels when a personal weakness is publicly revealed and when one is thinking irrationally.

When you feel ashamed, you try to avoid the company of people who know you well because you imagine that they will be making comments which 'belittle' you, or pour scorn on you for revealing your inadequacy and confirming your own view of yourself as a pretty hopeless individual.

How do you combat this tendency to see yourself as an inadequate person? First, you challenge and dispute the iB behind it until you no longer believe it. In other words, you tackle the belief: 'I must perform well and win the approval of important people in the organisation. If I fail to do well and win approval I am an inadequate person!' Now compare your challenges with those we suggested above. Do they match up? Secondly, replace that iB with the alternative rBs:

- 'I prefer to do well and win approval for my decisions because there are practical advantages in doing so. But I don't *have* to do well or win anyone's approval. Clearly, "have to's" and "got to's" imply a law of the universe, and if such a law existed I could hardly avoid succeeding in everything I tackled and I would be practically *guaranteed* to win the approval of everyone significant to me. Obviously no such law exists. It would be highly preferable for me to succeed and to win others' acclamation; preferable, but not mandatory!'

- 'There is not, nor ever can be, any evidence that I am an inadequate person for doing poorly. Nor can the fact that I performed poorly on one occasion ever prove that I can never do well in future. Can the past ever prove anything about the future? My past behaviour is no guarantee of my future behaviour. If it were, I would be obliged to go on repeating the same patterns of behaviour for the rest of my life. It is a verifiable fact that my future is not merely a repetition of my past. I cannot, therefore, be a total failure just because I fail at various times on important tasks. I cannot, therefore, be assessed as a hopeless failure or an inadequate individual on the basis of my poor performances. My acts are only aspects of me, not the whole of me. I can, therefore, accept myself as a fallible human being who may act inadequately on occasion. And the more I can learn from my past and present errors the fewer I am likely to make later on.'

Next, you can tackle your inference: 'Once my friends and others I know in the business world see that I am no good, they will remember it, and I'll never be able to face them again.'

First, recognise that it is an inference. It is unlikely that all your friends and business acquaintances are going to think that you are an utter idiot because you made a mess of a big deal and are going to remember it and talk about it for years to come. If one of your friends came a cropper over some big business deal would you denigrate the unfortunate person and refuse him or her even a word of sympathy or support?

But let's assume the worst. Let's assume that everybody thinks you are a hopelessly inept decision-maker and that they are all laughing behind your back. It's very unlikely, but just suppose that. Now, why do you have to go along with their negative evaluation of you? If they think that you are an inadequate individual does that make you one? If you accept that you, a person, are not just your acts, traits and performances, but a complex ongoing process, a fallible human being who can perform brilliantly one day and poorly another day, but who can never legitimately be given any kind of global rating, then you need never link your own self-assessment with that of anyone else. You are not responsible for the way the wheels go round in somebody else's head. If others rate you negatively that is their problem. You can objectively assess your behaviour, correct mistakes in your thinking and in your behaviour, but you need never put yourself down for acting badly even if others take a poor view of your behaviour.

Remember, whenever you feel ashamed or humiliated, look for the iBs which make you feel that way. Then vigorously and *persistently* challenge and dispute them until you see that it is not your action or some other person's response to it that upsets you but the way you think about it. The more you practise this the sooner you will reach a point where you can tolerate personally derogatory responses from others without unduly upsetting yourself over them.

Once you really convince yourself of these rational alternatives to your previous iBs, you can improve your decision-making ability, and nicely avoid becoming ashamed of yourself and putting yourself down if, as it may happen occasionally, your decision should turn out badly for you and/or your organisation.

Creativity

It is often fun to be creative, and financially and in other ways it can be rewarding. Creativity, of course, implies change, and change in turn implies risk. We have already dealt with some of the emotional blocks some people experience when trying to confront change, or manage change through taking actions designed to cope with it or adjust to it. We find, not surprisingly, that much of what we have been saying about healthy risk-taking applies equally well to becoming creative.

Overcoming blocks to creativity

Let us make one thing clear at the outset. This chapter is not about how to become creative. That is not our purpose. There are several fine books which aim to show you how to unlock your creative potential and start doing creative work. Two of these 'mental lock breakers' which we would recommend you to get hold of are by Buzan and Von Oech (see References). Reading these books could help to get you going and they are fun to read as well. You could also benefit from studying some of Edward De Bono's well-known books on lateral thinking.

Our purpose is in a way supplementary to these books by Tony Buzan and Roger Von Oech. Their aim is to unfreeze your habitual ways of thinking and stimulate you into seeing the world around you in different ways – ways you may never have thought of before. Our aim is to dynamite those psychological self-created roadblocks which inhibit or sidetrack you from doing what you want to do and which you are theoretically capable of doing. Intelligent and perceptive people seem to require some kind of vitally absorbing activity to remain fully alive and happy. Living essentially means doing, thinking, creating, loving. Spending too much time in relaxing pursuits or passive enjoyments leads to boredom and a sense of alienation. So how do we overcome inertia and become healthily absorbed in some creative activity?

In this section we shall attempt to identify what kind of thoughts, what sort of mental attitudes would be likely to inhibit the expression of creative ideas or strategies you might be considering. Perhaps you have thought up something original yourself; or maybe some promising ideas are simmering in your mind as a result of reading some of the stimulating material put forward by any one of the writers mentioned above.

Ideas that can block your creativity

Just when you find your creative juices beginning to flow, something begins to hold you back from expressing or developing your new ideas. What are some of the fears, the excuses, the rationalisations people offer to 'explain' their tendency to hold back from going ahead and trying out their innovative ideas or new ways of doing business? Let's examine some of these notions which dampen creative thinking and inhibit innovative action:

What might people think?

Some people are too scared to get out of established grooves of thinking and acting, at least in public, for fear of what people might think about their ideas. Being creative does sometimes mean doing things that may look foolish, even involving breaking established rules. You may wonder if you should allow yourself the privilege of stepping outside accepted boundaries, overturning hallowed procedures or presenting people with alternative ways of looking at the world – 'What will people say?'

Suppose that people do look at you askance or think you are a bit of an oddball because you have come up with an original proposal that you believe could revolutionise the way things are done in your organisation for the benefit of all concerned. You are convinced your ideas are feasible. So what if people think your ideas are crazy? What terrible thing could happen to you? You won't be flayed alive. You might well have been two centuries ago, but hardly in this day and age.

Aren't you creating your own turmoil by the way you evaluate other people's attitude towards you? At point A, you think that people are saying uncomplimentary things about your ideas and implying that you are not up to the job. At point C you feel embarrassed and ashamed. Your reaction is to hold back your creative suggestions, play them down. What would you be telling yourself at point B to create those feelings? Probably something like: 'I feel like an idiot when people tell me I'm talking nonsense, especially my peers. Maybe they're right, I must have their approval at least, or I'm a dead duck!' Thus you devalue yourself because you accept other people's negative evaluation of you and your ideas.

By now you may see how you could dispute the irrational ideas paraphrased above. Thus you could ask: 'If others think I'm foolish, does that make me foolish? I can only feel like an idiot if I think I am one, and obviously I don't think I am an idiot. Even if my ideas turn out to be foolish, how can that make me a fool? No way! My ideas and other attributes may be rated as good or bad, but my self cannot legitimately be rated in any way whatsoever. As for "needing" other people's approval, that is obviously nonsense. If it was the case that I must have others' approval then I would have it!'

The rational alternative would, we suggest, be along these lines: 'I would certainly prefer other people and especially my peers to see the possibilities arising from my innovative ideas because then I could expect some cooperation from them in testing my ideas. But if they don't see things my way, too bad! They are entitled to their opinions, as I am to mine. It would be nice to have others' approval but I certainly don't need it. And if my ideas turn out to be foolish on this occasion, that doesn't mean that I am foolish or that I can never come up with some good creative ideas some other time.'

If you stayed with these rBs you would feel regret that your creative suggestions were impracticable but you would not feel ashamed. Moreover, you would feel quite strongly motivated to see whether modifications to your earlier ideas might be more promising, and you would not feel inhibited about experimenting with still other novel approaches until you finally came up with something viable.

Men and women of vision are not usually accorded immediate acceptance of their new or strange ideas. Far from it! Darwin, the Wright Brothers, Brunel, Einstein, were all told that their ideas were nonsense or practically impossible. In virtually every profession, including our own, innovative practitioners are frequently ignored or treated with hostility until eventually through sheer persistence their ideas win acceptance. Even in this space-conscious age, the early proponents of rocket propulsion were told by 'respected scientific authorities' that their ideas wouldn't work: 'in the vacuum of space, rockets would have nothing to push against!' This was around 1938. Thirty-one years later, rockets landed a man on the moon.

The moral of this story is, if you come up with an interesting, innovative idea, don't be put off by being told that your idea is not the established way of doing things, or that it is probably impossible and that you are wasting your time. So, take heart! Don't be afraid to ask, 'What if ...?' If our visionary forebears had meekly accepted rejection when they presented their ideas to the world, we would all still be living in caves.

'It's too uncomfortable and too hard!'
It is sometimes uncomfortable stepping out of habitual ways of thinking. It does involve considerable effort, there is a lot of inertia to be overcome before we can look at things in a different light. So it's uncomfortable and involves effort to get out of a rut and to start playing with new ways of thinking about problems in the hope of discovering

some promising new approaches to solving them. But is it *too* uncomfortable, and is it *too* much effort to overcome the inertia and become creatively absorbed? Think carefully about what you mean when you say that something is *too* uncomfortable, or that attempting to do such-and-such is *too* hard. Aren't you telling yourself: 'I shouldn't experience so much discomfort or have to work so hard at stepping outside my accustomed ways of thinking in order to become creative'?

Now ask yourself: 'Where is the evidence for my belief that going beyond my accustomed ways of thinking is too uncomfortable and is too hard?' Does it not look as if we have here a variant of major iB No. 3 – viz.: 'Because I prefer pleasure to pain, life should arrange that I get what I want quickly and easily and without too much hassle and pain, and life becomes unbearable if it does not.'

If you believe that irrational idea (which millions do!) you will experience Low Frustration Tolerance (LFT). LFT is the primary cause of problems such as avoidance of hard work, and opting for short-term comfort at the expense of more strongly desired, long-term goals. It therefore makes good sense to thoroughly dispute these iBs until you really give them up and strongly believe and feel that they simply don't make sense.

So, returning to the question you asked above, you could answer your challenge as follows:

- 'There is no reason why I *must* not have to work hard at going beyond my habitual ways of thinking in order to look a problems in a different light. If hard work were not required becoming creative would be easy. But it's not easy, so I'd better acknowledge that if I want to become a more creative thinker and innovative executive I'd better buckle down to work hard and persistently until I achieve that goal.'

- 'How is it *too* hard for me to change my established patterns o thinking? It may be *very* hard but it is hardly impossible Calling it "too hard" means only that it is harder than I want it to be. This amounts to my saying that whatever I want to be easy must really be easy – and that is clearly ridiculous.'

- 'Of course, it is uncomfortable for me to change the thinking habits I've grown up with, but right now it *should be* uncomfortable – for that's the way it really is: truly uncomfortable. Complaining about it being uncomfortable won't make it any less so. Therefore I'd better accept that what exists exists and get on with it.'

Acquiring a rational view of creativity

If you vigorously persist at disputing those iBs which tend to hold back or block your creative impulse, you will acquire a more rational outlook which will help, rather than hinder you in your quest to become creative. Thus, you will come to believe:

- 'Becoming creative often means standing things on their head and putting forward ideas which may strike some people as foolish. But if others think of me as foolish, their negative evaluation need not affect me unless I take it seriously; nor need I allow the negative reactions of others to deter me from pursuing my creative goals. If some of my ideas at times turn out to be unhelpful I need not devalue myself, but instead I can learn from my errors and help myself to do better in future.'

- 'Becoming creative is not easy nor is there any reason why it should be. I can accept that hard and persistent work may be the only way more often than not to achieve creative solutions to both current and future problems.'

- 'Life may be uncomfortable initially as I struggle to abandon old habitual ways of thinking and try to overcome my inertia to develop new creative and innovative strategies. But it cannot be impossibly uncomfortable unless I convince myself that it is so by allowing LFT to gain the upper hand. Some degree of discomfort now is acceptable in order to realise the worthwhile gains that creative thinking can confer on me later.'

We have shown you in the paragraphs above the two main sources of the blocks to creative thinking. These stem from commonly held iBs which we identified and debated. We will now briefly mention two minor blocks to creativity which stem largely from the same iBs we have already discussed.

'I might be resisted'

This one at least has the merit of being true! The more creative or revolutionary your ideas are, the greater is the resistance you are likely to encounter to getting them accepted. As we mentioned above, practically all great innovators are resisted at first, and for the same reasons that block people from releasing their creative impulses: it is difficult to break out of established patterns of thinking and acting; and it is uncomfortable at first to get used to new ways which are radically different from the old familiar ways. Resistance may also be generated by people who think your ideas are dangerous, foolish, upsetting and so on.

If you fear possible resistance to your creative bents because your ideas could upturn certain time-hallowed ways your colleagues have become accustomed to, check your own thinking. Are you holding back because of others' negative evaluation of what you are doing? Study our remarks above on sticking to your guns and refusing to devalue yourself when other people denigrate you and your ideas. You could also check to see if LFT is present. Are you afraid of resistance because it would mean that you would have to work harder and experience a higher degree of frustration and inconvenience than you feel you 'ought' to have to put up with in order to get your creative ideas accepted? If so, track down your iBs. Then, once you have identified them, you can challenge and dispute them using the methods we have been showing you until you no longer believe them.

If you persist at disputing your iBs until they no longer dominate your thinking, you will acquire a new rational alternative outlook. Thus, if your ideas meet with resistance or derision, you can tell yourself and truly believe: 'I wish to develop my creative potential because

I value new ideas and because I want to try out innovative methods to resolve some current problems. If I succeed, fine! If I fail and incur criticism, I will listen to my critics without necessarily agreeing with them or putting myself down because of their negative attitude towards me. I can incorporate others' suggestions if they seem helpful, but if all else fails I can always go back to the drawing board and think again.'

I'm not creative

If this belief is holding you back from trying, ask yourself, how do you know you are not creative? Have you really tried to do something different, create something you never created before? Perhaps you made some attempts to be different and you were criticised or laughed at. Or maybe you thought that being creative would be easy and when you discovered that it wasn't, you said: 'Oh, it's too hard to think of anything original. I guess I'm not cut out for that sort of thing. I'd better leave this creative thing for other people to get into who are better at it.' Thus you cop out without ever really knowing what your creative potential might amount to.

Those creative writers we recommended at the beginning of this section would argue that most people have the potential to be creative to a greater degree than they ever imagined. It is unlikely that you have no creative ability whatever! Could it not be that you are opting out of trying because you subscribe to one or more variants of those prime iBs we identified in the paragraphs above as the real culprits which block and stifle the creative impulse?

Be honest with yourself, then if you suspect that you are allowing your iBs to interfere with your potential for originality in whatever field you are interested, challenge and dispute them until you no longer believe them. Then, use some of the wise advice you will find in those books we recommended at the beginning of this section. You may be glad you did when you discover that you can be far more creative than you previously thought!

Becoming vitally absorbed in creative thinking and working enthusiastically towards your goals is the hallmark of healthy risk-taking and healthy living. You may prefer to work alone, but you will quite often discover that creativity is something of a group process, rather than just a solo effort on your part. Advertising is probably a typical example. Brainstorming sessions allow one to get feedback on one's ideas. Other people can act as catalysts for the emergence of your own innovative ideas provided you don't allow an irrational fear of disapproval to inhibit you from expressing yourself.

Summary

- *All life involves risk; risk and change are inevitably part of life. We discussed the meaning of risk and identified various types of risk.*

- *We answered the question: 'What is a healthy risk?' After discussing what it means to take a healthy risk we focused attention on the things that can prevent you from taking a healthy risk. This led into a discussion of the fundamental causes of irrational decision-making.*

- *Two forms of irrational decision-making were targeted for detailed examination: indecision and impulsiveness. The main iBs underlying these irrational styles of decision-making were identified and disputed. We then suggested rational alternatives to the iBs and showed how a more rational outlook would facilitate taking difficult decisions and enable you to live with whatever consequences might emerge from your decisions.*

- *We briefly discussed the advantages of creativity and recommended you to study the books of three writers on how to become creative.*

- *We then drew attention to some of the main iBs which block and stifle your attempts to think creatively and impede you from realising the full benefit from any creative and innovative ideas you come up with.*

- *Using our A-B-C model, we showed how creativity-blocking iBs could be disputed and eliminated and replaced by rational alternative ideas which would help to release your creative impulses and stimulate new ideas.*

4

Overcoming Fear Of Disapproval And Criticism

We would hardly expect you or anyone else to be overjoyed at the prospect of being criticised at work for incompetent performance of your duties. None of us like being criticised or being disapproved of, and there are good reasons for this. We may miss a salary rise, or find ourselves transferred to less interesting work we may even be demoted.

While these and other penalties following disapproval or criticism of our performances at work may legitimately cause us realistic concern and motivate us to take steps to improve our work so as to avoid further criticism, they do not adequately account for the fear which grips some people when they are asked to explain their behaviour to their boss, for example. Even the thought of going up for their annual appraisement interview fills some candidates with severe apprehension.

Interestingly, it is not only the interviewee who feels nervous. We have known interviewers who looked distinctly uncomfortable when called upon to criticise some colleague's performance. These interviewers will resort to fudging and softening their critical comments in order to spare their interviewee, and presumably themselves, any possible embarrassment.

For these reasons we consider it worth while to devote a chapter to examining fear of disapproval and criticism. Our aim is to help people on the receiving end to respond rationally to active disapproval or criticism and also to help those individuals who fear lack of approval to avoid upsetting themselves when the approval they seek is not forthcoming. It will be helpful at this point to briefly distinguish the fear of active disapproval from the fear of not getting approval before going on to analyse these fears in detail.

Fear of disapproval and criticism

If you only fear active disapproval you would not be too concerned at mere lack of approval. Why? Because not getting approval is not the same as getting active disapproval. In other words, a neutral response would be OK; it wouldn't bother you.

Fear of not getting approval

If you don't get approval, but you believe you *have* to get it, you will experience emotional and behavioural problems. The main reason for this is that you have the iB: 'I need your approval' which we will discuss in a moment.

Let's now examine in more detail the origins of those fears concerning the possibility of your being actively disapproved of and criticised or the fears that you may receive no approval at all. Let's start with fear of active disapproval or criticism. Imagine yourself in front of your Chief Executive. He is spelling out why he is dissatisfied with your performance and he isn't pulling his punches.

At point A you are being critically appraised and your shortcomings are being itemised, one by one. At point C, you experience a strong feeling of shame. What would you be telling yourself at point B to create these negative inappropriate feelings? Probably your evaluative iB at point B would be a variant of major iB No. 1: 'I must not be disapproved of. If I am, I'm no good.' Expressed more comprehensively this iB says: 'I must do well and not be disapproved of by significant people. If I am disapproved of and my performance is criticised, that is awful and proves that I am no good.' When you are disapproved of and your performance is criticised by significant people whose approval you feel you absolutely must have, you feel ashamed because you then condemn yourself for having performed poorly. You also predict that these significant people are bound to think badly of you and you tend to agree with that perceived judgement. We hope you find this formulation more readily understandable.

As if that was not enough of a handicap, your iB that you must not be disapproved of or criticised will land you in even more trouble. For if you believe that you absolutely *must* do well at all times and not be disapproved of by those at the top of your organisation, then you are going to be in a state of perpetual or potential anxiety as you dwell on the ever-present possibility that one day you *won't* do well and *then* how will you feel when you are actively criticised by the Chief Executive or the Chairman and in front of heaven knows how many members of the Board?

Overcoming your shame and anxiety

How do you overcome those uncomfortable and unhelpful feelings of shame and anxiety? They do not inevitably follow when you find yourself on the receiving end of direct criticism or active disapproval. Even if the criticisms levelled at you have some substance and justification, you don't *have* to put yourself down and think you are just no good even if you agree that the criticism is valid.

By now, we would guess you know the answer – *dispute your iBs and replace them with rational alternatives*. So, you would begin by challenging and disputing the iB behind your shame and anxiety. The culprit here is the iB: 'I absolutely *must* do well and not be disapproved of or criticised by significant people in the organisation. If I am disapproved of and my performance is criticised, that is awful and proves that I am no good.' You go after that iB and vigorously and *persistently* challenge it *until you no longer believe it*. We have emphasised these last six words because it is of crucial importance that you *vigorously* and *persistently* challenge and dispute your iBs until you see that you simply cannot continue to believe them, and therefore give them up. A cursory reading of this book may enable you to understand on the intellectual level that the various iBs we have identified, challenged and disputed are, indeed, irrational and untenable. But, in the words of that popular 'soul' ballad, 'How deep does it go?'

Merely understanding is not enough, any more than understanding how to drive a car will make you a good driver. Only persistent practice at disputing and acting against your most deeply ingrained iBs and replacing them with their rational alternatives will you eventually reach a point where your iBs will largely lose their power to seriously trouble you. And as your rBs take root and become an integral part of your core belief system, your emotional and behavioural responses to life's problems and difficulties will tend to be much more healthy, reality-oriented, appropriate and helpful in enabling you to attain your personal and corporate goals with the minimum of wear and tear on your nervous system.

We have already shown you in Chapter 3 several examples of disputing major iBs in detail. Rather than repeat ourselves, we would like to draw your attention at this stage to the salient characteristics of practically any iB you are likely to encounter which could cause you problems if you were to strongly believe it. The main feature of all the iBs we have presented and analysed so far is the presence of an absolutist 'should', 'ought' or 'must'. We stress the *absolutist* use or meaning of these words because there is a quite normal legitimate way in which these words may be used. For example, when we use them in a conditional sense we can say: 'I ought to study this book if I wish to pass the exam'; 'I should take my umbrella if I wish to avoid getting soaked today'; and 'I must remember to buy the tickets by noon today if we intend going to the matinee this afternoon.' Your emotional problems derive from the way you use 'should', 'ought' or 'must': that is to say, laying unconditional *demands* upon yourself, other people, or the world in general.

So now, let's dispute the variant of iB No. 1. This is the iB underlying your fear of being actively disapproved or criticised. Here it is again: 'I *must not* be disapproved of. If I am I'm no good':

Question: Is there any evidence I can produce to prove that I must not be disapproved of or criticised?

Answer: No. I would certainly like to avoid being criticised because it is probably a disadvantage to me so far as achieving my goals is concerned. But I cannot rationally believe that because I would very much like something to happen or not to happen, as the case may be, my wishes *must* be fulfilled. I don't control the world!

Question: If I am disapproved of or criticised, how does that prove that I am no good?

Answer: It doesn't! My acts may be evaluated and awarded some kind of rating according to some arbitrary external standard. But I, a human being, am a complex ever-changing process who cannot legitimately be given a global or overall rating. My performances, my deeds, my traits are only aspects of me. They are not my totality.

While you are about it, you could take the idea that you *must* do well, and proceed to dispute it in the manner we showed you in Chapter 3.

You can legitimately prefer to do well because of the practical advantages you may derive from doing well. However, even if you do well, that will *not* necessarily mean that you will not be criticised; you may be criticised for not doing even better! So you see, you would do better to eliminate your irrational fear of criticism and disapproval at the source by tackling the iBs which give rise to it rather than try to sidestep the issue by laying this demand on yourself that you absolutely must do well in the hope that if you succeed you will avoid criticism. You might, but don't bank on it!

Once you clearly see why the various iBs you encounter make no sense and are likely to sabotage your best interests if you believe them, you can weaken their influence by working out rational alternative Beliefs and by persistently reminding yourself of them. Once these more rational philosophies become part of your basic belief system they will be much more likely to help you achieve your personal and corporate goals. If achieving peak performance is also your abiding aim, rational thinking will go a long way to help you achieve it.

Now, what *rational alternative Belief* would you hold in preference to the variant of major iB No. 1 which we have just shown you would lead to shame and anxiety? We would suggest the following rB: 'I much prefer not to receive active disapproval or criticism from significant people because in that way I am more likely to achieve my goals. But if I am criticised it will be unfortunate and possibly a setback to my ambitions but it will not be a personal tragedy or mean that I am no good. Also, by listening constructively to the criticisms I receive without putting myself down for being criticised, I can try to discover how I can rectify my mistakes or failings and learn to do better in future. My failures do not make me a worthless person. They mean only that I am a fallible human. By accepting myself with my failings I can strive to change what is in my power to change so that I can help myself to achieve more successes and fewer failures throughout the remainder of my career.'

If you truly believe these rational alternative Beliefs you would feel sorry and disappointed that you were criticised by significant people in the organisation, but you would not feel ashamed or depressed, and would feel motivated to take the criticisms of your performance as constructive ways of enabling you to focus on correcting your errors and to perform more satisfactorily in future.

You will recognise the analysis above as a further example of ego anxiety which you encountered in Chapter 3. Now let's look at some other reasons why people fear active disapproval and criticism.

Life must not be too hard!

That expression should sound familiar! As you may now have realised, the three major iBs are seldom encountered in their 'pure' or standard form. In practical situations, they appear as variants or derivatives of the standard form – as in the example above where we saw the emotional and behavioural results of subscribing to major iB No. 1.

Now, we have, under the above heading, a derivative of major iB No. 3: 'Because it is preferable that I experience pleasure rather than pain, the world absolutely should arrange this and life is horrible, and I can't bear it when the world doesn't.'

In the practical situation where you have received active disapproval and criticism of your performance, you are probably telling yourself a derivative of the above major iB like: 'Being criticised like this is terrible! Now my life is going to be much harder what with my having to re-cast all my department's plans and develop new work schedules. I'm going to have to spend goodness knows how many extra hours each week on meeting my deadlines. It isn't fair, and I can't stand being treated like this.'

The consequences of holding this iB are feelings of self-pity and resentment at being 'made' to do what you believe you shouldn't have to do. You are unlikely to determinedly push yourself to make the required changes in your work pattern and you may even sabotage your career by telling the boss he can stuff the job. Even if you resist that temptation, everything will seem to you much harder than it actually would be so long as you keep telling yourself: 'It shouldn't be so hard, and it's unfair!'

The more you dwell on the 'unfairness of life being so hard', the harder your job will seem to be. And the harder the job seems to be, the more you will dwell on how unfair life is for making things so hard for you. How does one resolve the problem? The answer is that you tackle it in the same way as you tackled the previous problems you encountered: challenge and dispute the iBs underlying your upset feelings and inappropriate behaviour and replace the iBs with rational alternatives.

Disputing irrational Belief No. 3

Question: Can I produce any real evidence that life should not be hard for me, and that the world must arrange it?

Answer: No. The facts speak for themselves. Life can be hard, and some people have it a great deal harder than others. If there was some law that the world must make life less hard for me, then life would be less hard. It could hardly be otherwise if such a law existed. Clearly such a law does not exist so it makes no sense to demand that it exists!

Question: Is it true that I *can't stand* it when the world treats me more harshly or less fairly than I would wish?

Answer: No. You obviously can stand it because you are standing it! You can stand anything until you are dead!

Now, consider the rational alternative Belief to 'Life must not be too hard!': 'Life may be hard for me at times and harder than I would like it to be, but there is no reason why it shouldn't be the way it indubitably is. So let me cut this nonsense about feeling sorry for myself because my life isn't presently as easy as I would like it to be and buckle down to doing something constructive to make things better for myself. Some hard work isn't going to make me fall apart at the seams and it could mean that if I put my back into making a success out of the criticisms the boss has given me, my life could be better for me in the future. So let's get going!'

Now, let's take a third situation where people fear active criticism and disapproval.

I must get what I want

Here we have another *demand*! In this case you fear that receiving active disapproval would mean that your promotion chances have been blocked, or that you were not going to receive that salary rise you had been banking on. So, you hold the iBs:

- 'I *must not* be criticised and blocked from getting what I must have because if I don't get promoted or the salary rise I want, then I'm no good!'

- 'I *must not* be criticised and blocked from getting what I must have because if I don't get promoted or the salary rise I want, I'd be deprived and I *can't stand* that!'

We imagine that you will easily recognise the first iB as another example of ego anxiety, and the second as yet another case of discomfort anxiety or low frustration tolerance (LFT), both of which you are by now familiar with. See if you can come up with rational alternative Beliefs to these two. Our suggestions are:

- 'I would much prefer not to be criticised, but if I am criticised for a poor performance or because the Chief Executive thought I could have done better and the promotion I expected is blocked and/or I don't receive that salary raise I expected, that is too bad. If my performance wins me only disapproval, I can hardly expect a bouquet! The fact of my performance being criticised doesn't mean that I am no good unless I myself foolishly think so. I am me, a fallible human being who on this occasion has failed to reach a certain standard and has been criticised. Tough! Now let me see how I can use this criticism to correct my shortcomings and do better next time.'

- 'I would much prefer not to be criticised because I very much wanted to win that promotion or at least a salary rise, but I didn't. So I'm deprived! My performance was criticised and I certainly don't like that, but I can obviously stand it. Maybe now I'd better sit down and figure how to profit from the criticisms I've received so that I stand a better chance of getting what I want in future.'

Now let's examine the fear of not getting approval, which, you will recall, we distinguished from fear of active disapproval or criticism.

When you don't get approval and you believe you need it

As we noted at the beginning of this chapter, if you only fear active disapproval you would not be too concerned at mere lack of approval. Why? Because not getting approval is not the same as getting active disapproval. However, if you don't get approval, but you believe you have to get it, you will experience emotional and behavioural problems. The main reason for this is that you have the iB: *'I need your approval'* which we will discuss in a moment. But you would also experience problems over not getting approval if your other major beliefs were: 'Life must not be too hard' (see p. 91 above); and 'I must get what I want' (see p. 92 above), since you see lack of approval as a threat to a relatively easy life in the first case and a threat to getting what you want in the second.

Let's first review these two iBs in the context of not getting approval but believing you need it.

Life must not be too hard

If you believe this, you will tend to look constantly for signs of approval because you are scared that if you don't get it you will have to work harder and/or longer hours to get the things in life you want fairly quickly and easily and which you insist *shouldn't* be too hard to acquire. Here is how to dispute this iB:

Question: If life would be harder for you if you fail to get approval from your boss, where is the evidence that it *should not* be hard? Just because you want certain things without having to work too hard to get them, must the world oblige by making you a special case?

Answer: There is no evidence that because we want something to be easy, therefore it must be. It would be nice if we could get what we wanted without too much effort or trouble. But if a thing is difficult, it's difficult. Tough!

Question: What would be a *rational alternative* in the present context to the iB, 'Life must not be too hard'?

Answer: Whether we like it or not, life can be, and often is, difficult. That's the way it is! If I encounter difficulty in getting some of the things I want from life, that is unfortunate and frustrating, especially if lack of approval from my boss has deferred my material advancement, and this in turn means I have to work harder. But it's not the end of the world and if working harder looks like being the answer, then I had better uncomplainingly do just that. If hard work is what it takes, that's the way it is. I may not like it at first, but I can certainly stand it.

I must get what I want

Suppose you are after promotion. You believe you absolutely must get it. You will then see lack of approval as meaning that you will be blocked from getting it now and/or in the future. Your iBs about this are either of the following:

- 'If I don't get approval for my work I won't get promoted and if I don't get promoted I'm no good' (If you believe that you experience ego anxiety.)

- 'If I don't get approval for my work I won't get promoted and if I don't get promoted I'd be deprived, and I *can't stand* that.' (If you believe that you experience discomfort anxiety.)

We suggest you review the previous section on fear of active disapproval or criticism. There you will find a comprehensive treatment of the iBs and their rational alternatives to the major iBs 'Life must not be too hard', and 'I must get what I want' which we repeated for your convenience in the present section (see pp. 94-5 above).

I need your approval!

If you have a dire need for someone's approval, whether it be at work or in your personal life, you obviously fear active disapproval and criticism. But you will also fear not getting any approval at all. So let us take a closer look now at the third major reason why some people have a fear of not getting approval.

What do you think the major iBs are in the case of someone who thinks he or she needs the approval of some significant person in his or her life in order to be happy? Obviously, it is iB No. 1 which is probably becoming familiar to you: 'I must win the approval of important people. If I don't, I am an *inadequate person!*' This major iB can take several forms or variants in your working environment. For example, you will hear: 'I must get *some* appreciation from my boss for all the work I do here. If I don't, that means I'm not much good!'

These ideas are irrational and self-defeating for two reasons:

- You may not be doing badly at all but still fail to receive appreciation or approval because your boss doesn't believe in handing out praise. He will readily criticise your work if he thinks it isn't up to scratch but otherwise he is as silent as the Sphinx.

- Your boss may be loathe to praise you in case you become complacent and stop trying as hard as you used to.

Regardless of whether these reasons apply in any given case, your best bet is to give up the belief that you must be given some proof of approval, or else you are an inadequate person. The reason for saying that is this: if you convince yourself that you *must* have someone's approval, firstly you are going to upset yourself over the fact that you are not getting approval, and secondly you are likely to do all the wrong things to try to get it, as we shall show you in a moment.

Tackling the dire need for approval

Using the disputing techniques with which we expect you are now familiar, you could proceed as follows to demolish the silly notion that you are nothing unless you have the approval of some person who is important to you:

Question: Why *must* I get approval from important people?

Answer: There is no reason why I *must* get approval although it would be *desirable* because of the practical advantages to be gained from winning the approval of people who can influence my future career.

Question: If I fail to get approval for my performance does that prove that I am an inadequate person?

Answer: It proves no such thing! Even if I do not perform well and fail to get approval, I am hardly an *inadequate person* but a *person* who performed inadequately on this occasion but who can learn to do better in future.

Question: Just because I failed – for whatever reason – to get some approval for my work from my boss, does that prove I'll *never* get approval from anyone for whom I work?

Answer: Not at all! That is a silly over-generalisation. If I keep trying, it is unlikely that I'll never win approval from anyone I might work for. But even if I never get approval from anyone, I can still accept myself because my worth or value to myself does not depend upon whether others like me or approve of me. While I definitely *prefer* to receive some degree of approval because of the possible advantages that can come from it, I definitely don't *need* it.

If you dispute those iBs which create the feeling that you *need* approval and that you are no good without it, you will probably become much less obsessed with continually looking for evidence of 'Am I getting approval, am I getting approval?' and more concerned with doing the best job of which you are capable and then seeing what feedback you are getting. If you receive promotion or the salary increases commensurate with the value of your work, the degree of verbal approval you get, or don't get, will not then seem all that important to you.

Be true to yourself

However, if you are still carrying around this dire need for approval you will tend, as we pointed out already, to do all the wrong things to get it. Thus, you will set out to be nice and helpful to everybody who matters to you in the hope that they in turn will reward you by giving you what you want. This may work in the short term but usually fails in the longer term. When you become other-directed you tend to concentrate on pleasing others instead of attending to what you really want to get for yourself. In a sense you are acting dishonestly by pretending you are only out to please others when you are really hoping that they will 'reward' your boot-licking by giving you what you want. Sooner or later your plan will backfire because people will see through you or suspect your motives. Others will simply take advantage of you and feel no obligation to do anything for you. 'Be true to yourself' is a wise maxim worth remembering and living by.

If fear of not getting approval is a problem for you, tackle your underlying iB that you are no good unless you have others' approval. You don't have to be outstanding in order to accept yourself. Give yourself unconditional self-acceptance, figure out what you really like doing in life. What do you enjoy? When you know what your goal is, go for it and don't think you have to have anybody else's approval before you can accept yourself or allow yourself to strive for what you really want from your life. You will more readily win the respect of other people if you show them that you respect your own rights first. You can still show care and concern for others and even put their wishes first some of the time, but unless you are dedicated to the service of others you would be unwise to slavishly try to win their approval in the hope of getting your own wishes satisfied.

The rational alternative to needing approval

If you study the rational answers we offered for your consideration in the disputations in both this and the previous sections, you should now be able to suggest rational alternative Beliefs to replace those iBs which previously created the fear you may have experienced when you don't get approval from significant people in your organisation. Thus, you could believe: 'It's nice to receive approval, at least some of the time because getting such approval, especially from those important people in the organisation who can influence my career, can often lead to advancement and other benefits. But I don't absolutely need such approval and there is no reason why I must get it because I would prefer it. If lack of approval from my boss seems to be correlated with lack of progress in my career, I can objectively check this out by enquiring if my performance on the job meets the standard expected of me. If I have failed to perform adequately, that is too bad, and could be a setback to my career, at least temporarily, but it doesn't mean that I am a total failure, but only a person who has failed on this occasion. I can accept myself with my shortcomings and determinedly take appropriate steps to recover lost ground and to do better in future.'

If you can make these rBs your own deeply held convictions you may feel disappointment when you fail to receive expressions of approval from those above you after you have done a reasonably good job, but you won't feel 'hurt' or angry over not getting such approval.

Some comments on criticism

When discussing various rational alternative Beliefs in previous sections, we have drawn attention to the point that you can often benefit from being criticised if you view the occasion as providing you with useful feedback on how you could improve your ideas and/or performance. The point to remember is that you can do this once you realise that any criticism you receive can be a criticism only of your ideas, or deeds or performances – never of you as a person. This follows from our contention which we have reiterated throughout that we can only legitimately rate a person's deeds, traits and behaviours – never the person him or herself.

Criticism can be helpful

When you receive criticism, ask yourself, what is being criticised? If you are offered vague generalities, such as 'you'll never change', seek clarification. Ask the interviewer to be specific. 'What is it about me that you think will *never* change? Why do you think that?' These questions are examples of what we mean.

If specific points are raised about your performance, for example, and put forward for you to consider in an intelligent manner, welcome them! Once you take the alleged 'horror' out of being criticised, you will realise that intelligent criticism can benefit you. It gives you an opportunity to see how others objectively view your performance and potential for future progression and can help you to change those aspects of your performance or attitude which are seen as unhelpful to you.

If words like 'hopelessly incompetent' or other obviously self-rating expressions are used against you, swallow your displeasure and try to get your interviewer to be more specific and say *exactly* what he or she means. Try not to let your interviewer get away with over-generalisations. You could say: 'What leads you to conclude that . ..'; 'Is it completely bad that ...'; or 'Is there nothing at all praiseworthy about my performance over the past year?'

Being oversensitive

If you are oversensitive to criticism you will tend to overestimate the extent or the severity of the criticisms you receive. Your attitude influences the way you interpret criticism. You may even see criticism where none was intended. We once knew a woman who had a positive talent for taking practically anything that was said to her and somehow finding a hidden critical meaning in it. Such people usually have a very low opinion of themselves and imagine that others agree with it.

If you suspect you are oversensitive, how do you see yourself? Perhaps you have a low opinion of yourself, a low level of self-acceptance. If that should be a problem, look for the iBs you hold about yourself. Search out your unconditional 'shoulds', 'oughts' and 'musts' in the context of the three major iBs you now have studied, particularly No. 1!

Rationally handling appraisement interviews

If you have understood us so far, your knowledge and understanding of Rational-Emotive Training will stand you in good stead when you come up for an appraisement interview.

These appraisements, usually conducted annually, go beyond the day-to-day criticisms of some of your specific decisions or actions by your immediate superiors. The annual appraisement attempts to provide you with an overall assessment of your ability and your potential for further progress up the organisation. If you go into these appraisement interviews with the rational conviction that you can learn something useful from them, you will be concerned but not unduly upset by disapproval or criticism, nor will you view it as a catastrophe if your interviewer does not share your view that your performance over the past few months is already pointing you towards the leadership of the organisation! What you will be looking for is constructive, objectively offered, verifiable criticism. The better interviewers will often be helpful to you if you listen carefully to what they are trying to convey to you. That should be their purpose if they are up to their job. Human resources are too valuable to waste, especially at your level.

In the space available, our comments must necessarily be brief. However we hope to make two useful points. *Interviewers are human*, and therefore are fallible like the rest of us. No one on this planet is annointed with rationality! Some interviewers may be reluctant to give praise even when your performance has merited it. If you receive nothing but negative criticism, you may be facing an interviewer who considers that giving ostensible approval or praise is tantamount to encouraging you to be less careful, less painstaking, or not working as hard as you might. Such people tend to be perfectionists and seem to expect you to be likewise. In Chapter 2 we endorsed perfectionism as an objective to aim at in your work performance but counselled against using the drive towards perfectionism as a device to raise your 'ego' by rating your *self* as perfect when you actually *do* exceptionally well. Some interviewers may make this irrational identification and view you and your acts as being the same thing. They may consequently strive to avoid giving you too high an opinion of yourself should you have achieved some outstanding performances in case it encourages you to rest on your oars and do less well in future. Knowing this, you can make allowances by recalling our treatment of the iB, 'I need your approval', and not permit yourself to be unduly dismayed by your interviewer's lack of expressed approval for your meritorious deeds!

Normally, interviewers will not be backward in coming out with criticisms of your performances and abilities. However, you may encounter some who are somewhat inhibited about being too directly critical, their fear being that you will feel 'hurt' if they are too direct in their criticisms. So they tactfully soft-pedal their comments and criticisms, hoping that you won't feel 'offended'. Here, the error is the opposite of the error made by the perfectionist. The former errs by being over-critical, the latter by not being critical enough. Both implicitly believe that you are the same thing as your deeds and traits and that your view of yourself, your so-called 'self-image', will reflect the type of critical assessment you receive.

When your interviewer is too 'nice' and you perceive that he or she thinks criticising your performances is the same thing as criticising you as a person, he or she may overcompensate by giving you more praise than your record merits. In neither case are you being clearly shown where your strengths and weaknesses really lie. You can help put matters into perspective in this case by showing your interviewer that you do not put yourself down or consider yourself an inadequate person because your attention has been drawn to your failings in some particular area. Thus, you could say: 'You know, I think I really messed up badly on that particular project you recall I was working on last year. When all I got from the Chief Executive was a fairly mild reprimand – well, mild by his standards, I guess I got off lightly. Wouldn't you agree?' By unashamedly acknowledging your own failures and shortcomings you may help your appraisement interviewers to be more forthcoming with their assessment and criticisms of your overall performance and potential. *Your objective* should be to make each appraisement interview a useful learning experience for you. And if your appraisement interviewers can learn something useful to help them do their job better, so much the better!

Our final point is this: our ideas, our performances can be criticised. They can be rated good, bad or indifferent. That's OK. We can learn a lot of useful things from good feedback. Do not overestimate the extent of expressed disapproval or criticism. Your attitude influences your interpretation and if you are oversensitive you will tend to miss the good part of the criticism you are receiving because you will no longer be really listening to it instead you will be dwelling on the 'terrible' things you think are being said about *you*! Remember to focus on 'what is being criticised'. If you are called incompetent or a hopeless individual, your critic is wrong because total *self-rating*, as we have emphasised throughout this book is not legitimate. There's no need to be afraid of intelligent appraisal and criticism. Once you take the 'horror' out of being criticised, even severely criticised, then intelligent criticism can be a good thing for you if you use it appropriately to achieve and maintain your peak performance. That's your goal, isn't it?

Summary

- *We began by identifying two aspects of fear of disapproval and criticism. We distinguished fear of active disapproval and criticism from the fear of not getting approval.*

- *We identified the salient iBs which create fear of disapproval and criticism and outlined rational alternative beliefs which would help you to understand and profit from intelligent criticism.*

- *We set out the reasons why some people feel they need others' approval and how they needlessly upset themselves when approval is not forthcoming. The relevant iBs were identified and rational alternatives were suggested.*

- *Various types of criticism and how to respond to them were discussed. We showed how criticism could be viewed as helpful when offered and responded to in an intelligent and rational manner.*

- *Oversensitivity to criticism was shown to be likely to encourage interviewees to misinterpret the extent and severity of criticisms they might receive. Steps to overcome this handicap were outlined.*

- *We concluded the chapter by looking at some of the errors made in appraisement interviews. We made the point that interviewers might hold certain irrational ideas of their own which could influence the way in which they conducted their appraisements, and showed you how to be alert to this possibility and to spot the likely underlying iBs.*

- *We suggested rational ways of handling the situation if you were confronted with excessively negative criticism on the one hand, and on the other hand how to respond rationally if your interviewer seemed to be unduly playing down the more critical points in your overall performance assessment.*

5

Overcoming Procrastination

As an executive you know that effective executive functioning depends on effective control: control of your time, control of your subordinates and of their time. You know what needs to be done, how it has to be done and when it has to be done. Your subordinates depend on you to tell them what to do. You determine their objectives.

So, let's assume your goal is to lead your organisation. You have mapped out for yourself a strategic plan and the shortest practicable route to your goal, and you are single-mindedly determined to achieve it. You hope you have that extra quality that will give you that vital edge over the competition that will earn you acceptance as a true leader and not just in name only.

Your management training and your experience all count towards helping you reach your chosen goals. However, before you begin to control your organisation and the way it works, you need a large degree of self-regulation. In other words, you need a large measure of self-discipline, and unless you have that you are unlikely to get very far in becoming a highly effective executive.

Our aim is to help to prepare you. There is no question that you know precisely what you want to do. You know that working hard and persistently is essential if you are ever to come within sight of achieving your personal and organisational goals. Knowing what you want, you are willing to devote yourself to achieving it, to think and act and to willingly sacrifice, at least in the shorter term, many of the good things and pleasurable activities that others around you devote their lives to seeking and enjoying.

Overcoming the barriers

So far OK! But it is not quite as easy as just knowing where you want to be in a few years time and devoting your time and efforts to getting there. You know there are barriers to overcome, problems to be solved, difficulties to be surmounted. That is your job – solving problems and discovering the most efficient way to enable you and your department to reach your targets. Life is full of hassles and frustrations as you know from experience.

But what about those other inner urges, those strings which seem to suddenly appear and tie you down, those *irrational notions* which occasionally take hold and interfere with your better judgement, those unrealistic demands which you impose on yourself and others which impede you in the pursuit of your dearest wishes? These are the roadblocks, the inner obstacles which Rational-Emotive Training brings to your awareness. Your management training and experience equip you to deal adequately with the everyday problems and hassles which are an integral part of the life of an executive today. Rational-Emotive Training equips you to recognise and break down those inner barriers to functioning at your optimum level of executive efficiency and opens the way forward to the attainment of your cherished desires and goals. Let's take a close look now at one of the chief culprits around which, if you let it, will do its best to see to it that you never accomplish your most important desires and objectives. Its name is procrastination.

Procrastination: what is it?

Procrastination doesn't just mean putting off doing something until a later time. You might want to defer taking a decision, for example, because you need more data before taking any action. Or, you could put back acting on a particular decision because a more urgent or important problem has arisen which justifies your immediate attention. There are all sorts of rational reasons you might have for postponing until tomorrow something you had intended doing today.

What we mean by procrastination is this: you continue to put off, and put off taking some decision or action which you know darned well had better be done now, pronto, but which you refuse to carry out for a number of highly irrational reasons.

When you procrastinate by putting off some task which you know had better be done promptly, you are the victim of one or more of these irrational ideas which literally millions of people believe:

- You are afraid that you won't do well and that you *have* to do well. If you don't do well, you would damn yourself for not living up to your standards and so you put off the feared event to avoid the ego anxiety associated with it.

- You fear that if you don't do well, you will be disapproved of and criticised by others. And because you think that you *must* do well, the possibility that you won't, fills you with ego anxiety.

- *'It's too hard!'* This is your old 'friend' whom you have met on a number of previous occasions, and whom you haven't seen the end of just yet. Do you recognise the major iB involved here? If not, read on!

- You feel resentment at being asked to do something you don't want to do, and think you shouldn't have to do. You feel imposed upon, but because you feel too scared to confront the person concerned, you hit back by means of some sort of passive-aggressive behaviour such as taking much longer than you need to carry out the requested task, or even not doing it at all.

We will examine presently in detail each of these 'reasons' for procrastinating. Before we do so, however, we want to ask you a question. It is this: *Is it in your interest to overcome procrastination?* You might think this is a silly question to ask. 'After all,' you might say, 'If procrastination leads to loss of valuable time – a precious commodity which once lost can never be replaced – and in consequence leads to loss of money, and, as you claim, lowers our executive efficiency and puts a question mark over the prospect of achieving our valued executive desires and goals, why should we not want to overcome it? Surely it is in our best interests to rid ourselves of our procrastinating propensities?'

Our reply would be: 'Yes, we think it would be in virtually everyone's best interests to overcome their procrastination tendencies. But to do so requires real determination and effort. To succeed, you will often find you have to sacrifice present comforts for longer term gains. But disciplining yourself to do just that is your problem! If you rebel against having to carry out some important but onerous or boring task because it is more personally enjoyable to do something else instead, you may wonder what the point is in trying to overcome procrastination if that means having to endure present pain for future gain. You may think it is like trying to pull yourself up by your bootstraps!'

What is our aim?

Our aim is to convince you that it will definitely be worth your while to overcome procrastination. You don't have to, of course. Life will still go on; procrastinating isn't the worst problem you could experience. But, the benefits from overcoming this very prevalent, self-defeating behaviour are considerable and extend far beyond helping you achieve your peak performance as an executive. People who root out their procrastination problems enjoy unexpected side benefits and help themselves to lead more satisfying lives. If we can assume that you are willing to give it an honest try, we invite you now to examine with us the basic causes of procrastination. Then we will give you some sound, reality-tested advice on how to rid yourself of it.

Procrastination: what causes it?

We have already drawn your attention briefly to the four basic causes of procrastination. We will now examine each of them in turn in more detail. As you may suspect, procrastination, like virtually any other dysfunctional behaviour, stems from one or more major iBs. So, taking them in the same order as we briefly introduced them above, we can pinpoint a derivative of iB No. 1: 'I must do well and live up to my standards. If I don't I rate as a no-good person!' The emotional consequence of holding that iB is anxiety. Since you experience anxiety as an uncomfortable feeling, you try to avoid the feeling by postponing for as long as you can, the action you believe (erroneously) will cause the anxiety.

To take an example: your boss has asked for a detailed breakdown of the expenditure you incurred on a project you were given responsibility for implementation. At the time, this should have been carefully monitored, but it wasn't because certain aspects were overlooked due to the absence of two individuals who normally would have carried out the monitoring. In consequence, the information you have available is incomplete and therefore your report will be incomplete. Acknowledging your lapse of control over what was going on in your department and submitting only a partial account of the expenditure, suitably qualified of course, would constitute a less than perfect production. So you invent some specious, but plausible reasons for not being able to submit the fully detailed report that was asked for.

Even if you get away with it this time, so long as you hold the iB that you *must* do well, and that if you fail to live up to your high standards you are no good, you will experience more anxiety the next time you fail to turn in a less than perfect job.

We have already disputed the irrationality of iB No. 1 in previous chapters in considerable detail. If you are not too sure of the reasons why they were irrational we suggest you go back to Chapter 4 and review what we said there. For your convenience we have highlighted iB No. 1 in its complete or standard form in the box below.

Major irrational Belief No. 1

Because it would be highly preferable if I were outstandingly competent and/or loved, I absolutely should and must be; it's awful when I am not, and therefore I am a worthless individual.

What rational alternative Belief could you justifiably hold in preference to iB No. 1? We suggest: 'I much prefer to do well and reach as high a standard of excellence as I can in my work because I can achieve my goals and improve my prospects of advancement. But there is no reason why I absolutely have to do well, and if I don't do as well as I am theoretically capable of doing, that is unfortunate and possibly a setback, but hardly a catastrophe. I can accept the consequences of my failure on this occasion without devaluing myself as a human being, and learn from my experience how to avoid making a similar mistake in future.'

If you believed that and acted upon it, you would not postpone handing in your report because it was incomplete. Instead, you would openly acknowledge and accept responsibility for the failure and take action to ensure that the error would be unlikely to happen in future. Your feeling would be one of regret over having allowed the mistake to happen and you would lose no time in taking corrective action to avoid making that mistake again.

Now, let's examine the second basic cause of procrastination. Like the first example, it stems from an iB: *You fear that if you don't do well, you will be disapproved of and criticised by others.* And because you think that you must do well, the possibility that you won't fills you with ego anxiety.

Once again, if you look closely, you can spot the major iB. It is in fact No. 1 which we highlighted in the previous section. Its variant in this case is: 'I must do well and not be criticised by people who matter to me. If I fail to do well and others criticise me, that proves I'm no good.'

So, you fear being criticised if you don't perform well, because of the low opinion you think others will have of you and which you agree with. So you procrastinate by not handing in that report, or handing it in late, so that your low performance assessment will look as if it stemmed from your lateness rather than from an inadequately presented report. By doing nothing to tackle your underlying iBs, you do nothing to break your propensity to become anxious at the prospect of not doing well and being criticised. In consequence, continuing to procrastinate may serve you as an 'out', a way of avoiding an unpleasant situation, but it will have cumulative disadvantages for you which will do nothing to advance your career, and may even set it back.

A rational alternative Belief to fear of disapproval

If you dispute the major iB which creates your fear of criticism and disapproval as we have shown you previously, and especially in Chapter 4, you would reach a more rational view of your situation if you did, in fact, incur some criticism and disapproval for having acted incompetently. Thus, you could convince yourself of the following: 'I prefer to do well and to avoid criticism, especially from my superiors, for practical reasons; it does my career prospects no good. But if I am criticised for some failure on my part, that is unfortunate and I won't like it, but I am not an inadequate person for having failed but only a person who has acted inadequately and who can learn from experience to correct my failings and to do better in future.'

Your would feel sorry and regretful for having made a mistake and picked up a reprimand but you would feel determined to take whatever action was necessary to avoid making a similar mistake again and to do better generally as far as possible. Without a feeling of anxiety at the possibility of failure in future you would not be motivated to procrastinate in order to cover up the discomfort associated with anxiety.

'It's too hard!'

This is in our view the major and most common cause of procrastination. It is a direct derivative of major iB No. 3. We think it worth while to highlight it for you here seeing it is, unfortunately, so widely believed.

Major irrational Belief No. 3

Because it is preferable that I experience pleasure rather than pain, the world absolutely should arrange this and life is horrible, and I can't bear it when the world doesn't.

Because it is preferable that I experience pleasure rather than pain, the world absolutely must arrange this and life is horrible, and I can't bear it when the world does not.'

Now if you believe that, you will certainly have a low tolerance of frustration. Low frustration tolerance (LFT) is at the root of several related problems, such as overeating, over-indulgence in alcohol and drugs and avoidance of hard work. Not only is LFT a direct cause of procrastination, it also exacerbates and sustains emotional disturbance in general. Take, for example, the two illustrations we offered you above of fear of not living up to one's high standards, and fear of getting disapproval or criticism. We showed you there how procrastination served to 'protect' you from the pain of facing up to your anxiety when you were afraid you would fail to do well. In the short term you avoided the pain of discomfort only to ensure you would suffer even more pain later and continue to do so until you took the bull by the horns and tackled the root of the problem. With LFT, you would convince yourself that it was 'too hard' to undertake the work necessary to deal with your anxiety and the discomfort associated with it. You tend to convince yourself: 'I find it too hard to bear! Even if the pain is of short duration, that is still too much, and I must avoid it at all costs!' So, you not only tend to prolong indefinitely your anxieties over failing to perform outstandingly and being criticised for not doing well enough, but your LFT constitutes the main and most direct cause of your procrastination. This is how it works.

LFT in action

You have submitted plans to your Board for an increase in your department's budget. You are taking on more people and believe you have justified your action. The Board are not convinced that you have made your case for an increase in the staffing level and they have sent back your proposals asking for a more detailed analysis to be done. They want it by last week, but they are prepared to settle for it not later than Monday next, by 09.30 sharp.

'This is too much!' you tell yourself and anyone who is prepared to listen will sympathise with you. 'It took me hours of extra work – most of it tedious repetitive stuff, to get that plan prepared, and now they want it virtually redone but with a lot of extra data which will mean even more work, and they want it by Monday next! I deserve *better* than this!'

The iBs here are fairly obvious, wouldn't you agree? You start off with a fairly rational Belief: 'Because I find certain aspects of preparing this plan boring and repetitive, I don't like these aspects. I wish I didn't have to do these rather dull calculations.'

So far so good. There is no reason why you should like doing what you find boring or unpleasant. But at this point you make what we call in Rational-Emotive Training a magical jump. You make certain other statements which go beyond the realm of reality and which cannot be proved or disproved, for example:

- 'Things I don't like doing shouldn't have to be done!'

- 'Because there are so many tedious calculations to re-check I can't possibly enjoy doing *any* of this submission the Board have asked for.'

- 'The way I am treated here, my life is *too hard*!'

- 'I *can't bear* going through all this work for a second time! Why the hell *couldn't* they accept my first draft plan? There wasn't much wrong with it!'

Can you see that all or these iBS are derivatives of major iB No. 3? If you think about them, none of these statements accords with reality. The essence of LFT can be summed up this way: 'If something exists that I consider undesirable but which I can't avoid if I'm to achieve my goals, then it ought not to exist and I can't stand it if it does!'

We recommend that you practise your by now considerable disputing skills on unravelling the over-generalisations, the illogical and unrealistic statements contained in these iBs we've just presented. There are many more like them and it will help you to recognise them as iBs whenever you come across examples. You could also devise some rational alternative Beliefs to replace the above iBs.

A rational alternative Belief to 'It's too hard'

'I have to re-draft my budget proposals and provide more data to satisfy the Board that the increased staffing level I want is justified. What a drag! Just when I thought that was it, back it comes and I have to do it again. Tough! If it has to be done, it has to be done. That's what I'm here for- to draw up proposals to help the business work more efficiently. I don't like some of the work, it's a bit of drudgery in places, but I can enjoy doing other parts of the work, so let me get on with it. It would be nice if everything I proposed went sailing through at the first attempt. But the Board have their job to do too, and if they are dissatisfied with my first attempt, they are dissatisfied! It is a hassle that I have to re-submit my proposals, but that's all it is, an inconvenience, so the sooner I get on with it the better. And if I do a good job on this one it might not do my promotion chances any harm either!' With that rB you would be self-motivated to buckle down to your task in spite of its tacky bits, and you would feel good about doing the best job you could since you see it is in your best interests to do so. Keeping in mind that example of LFT for further consideration, let's turn now to the fourth cause of procrastination.

Resentment

You feel resentment at being asked to do something you don't want to do, and think you shouldn't have to do. You feel imposed upon, but because you feel too scared to confront the person concerned, you hit back by means of some form of passive-aggressive behaviour such as taking much longer than you need to carry out the requested task, or even not doing it at all.

First, you hold a fairly rational Belief about being asked to resubmit your proposal to the Board: 'What a nuisance that I am asked to re-do my budget proposals! I wish the Board hadn't asked me to do it again. It means a lot of extra work for me, some of it quite tedious and uninteresting. But they have a right to ask for more information from me. They have a duty to their shareholders to make the business profitable and it's their job to scrutinise proposals for an increased budget for extra staff and to reject anything they are not happy with.'

But instead of getting on with it, and re-submitting your proposals with carefully constructed arguments supported by facts and figures, you rebelliously procrastinate in protest at being asked to do it. Why? Because you hold certain iBs and have a low level of frustration tolerance. In this instance you are probably telling yourself:

- 'Those Board members who make me go through all those tedious calculations just to please them are rotten people with no consideration for anybody!'

- 'Because they behave like this to me, they ought to drop dead!'

- 'Because they treat me so unfairly, I won't re-do that budget proposal even if I am reprimanded for it!'

- 'Maybe I could do the report again but make it clear to the Board that it's going to take me such a long time to complete it that they'll feel sorry and realise they have treated me unjustly.'

- 'If I can make them see how unfairly they have treated me, maybe other people in the organisation won't be imposed on in future and will be grateful to me!'

With absurd notions like these in control, you would not only procrastinate but probably be demoted, or even fired! Your self-righteous indignation-fuelled refusal to do something you vehemently believe you shouldn't be asked to do may make you feel good in the short term, but the likelihood is that you will have to cut off your nose to spite your face. Very silly and unprofessional behaviour!

Alternatively you could replace these highly self-defeating iBs with some rBs along the following lines: 'I admit it's a drag to have to re-submit these proposals of mine to the Board because they were unable to accept the first draft. But if they were unacceptable then the Board were right to refer them back to me for further consideration. They are not rotten people who are trying to impose on me but only people who have been appointed to run the organisation and it is not being unfair to me to ask me to support my budget proposals with more data. I don't like having to do it over again, but it's only an inconvenience, not a holy horror. So, let me get on with it and show the Board I know what I'm doing and that I can be trusted to do a responsible job.'

You will realise that expressing resentment or hostility to the Board is highly irrational if you are really serious about making it as a top-flight executive. You may legitimately disagree with some decisions, for example, and you can hold your ground on matters of principle, but it is highly self-defeating to allow yourself to peevishly resent doing work you are expected and paid to do and to resort to procrastination to 'get even' with those you irrationally believe are treating you unfairly. We will now outline some other approaches to help you overcome procrastination.

Overcoming procrastination

Prioritise your tasks

One way of helping yourself to cope with work which tends to pile up is to give a priority rating to those jobs which are obviously time-limited. Identify a series of tasks by allocating them tags; a, b, c, etc. Choose jobs which are important to tackle early and after giving them an appropriate priority rating, work on each one for as long as feasible. It isn't necessary to finish a given task at one fell swoop! Better to do something to get it going rather than do nothing at all and watch the pile of 'work waiting' grow deeper each day. You may seldom or never enjoy the luxury of having large blocks of time at your disposal to concentrate wholly on some important matter. If you keep putting off tackling a job until you do see yourself with loads of time to devote to it, you may never do it!

Time-tabling

Used in conjunction with task prioritisation, setting time limits to the amount of work you do on each task will enable you to whittle down large or incomplete tasks to manageable chunks. If you begin to procrastinate because you see a large project waiting to be started and you have little time left to do anything on it, make a start, however small it may be. Then you will see that you have at least made a start. You may even find that once you start it, you get into the swing of it and accomplish more than you thought you could.

The five-minute plan is another device you can use as part of your time-tabling strategy. You start a project and agree to spend five minutes with it. At the end of the five minutes you ask yourself: 'shall I give it another five minutes?' If you are like most people, you will probably decide to give yourself a further period of five minutes. Why? Because once you force yourself to get started initially, the impetus you have acquired during the first five minutes will often be sufficient to carry you on for a further five minutes – and another five and so on. You don't have to carry on beyond your original time period, but on occasion you may find it useful to let your natural tendency to continue along a path you have already chosen to carry you on to achieve your goal.

The use of rewards and penalties

Contingency management

Let's assume you want to perform some task but you don't feel like it and you keep foolishly putting it off. You ask yourself: 'What do I enjoy doing frequently?' Your answer could include things like listening to music, reading a favourite magazine, going out for a meal, or something else you particularly enjoy. Then you contract with yourself to work so many hours each day on your project and reward yourself with your desired activity *only* after you have spent the agreed amount of time on the project. Don't reward yourself *before* you do the stipulated work you have promised yourself. No work done, no reward! If you are afraid of cheating on yourself, get a friend to monitor you. If you apply this technique conscientiously you will find that this kind of reinforcement will not only help you to stop procrastinating; it will make you want to stop procrastinating. But you must do it conscientiously and regularly if you want to get the full benefit from it.

The use of penalties

If after contracting with yourself to spend a minimum amount of time each day on your project, you find yourself failing to do it in spite of the presence of potential rewards, you could try penalising yourself. Select some activity you particularly dislike, such as cleaning the bathroom. Then if you fail to put in the minimum time you have contracted to spend on your work, you clean your bathroom for at least half an hour! Another penalty you could award yourself would be to donate a sum of money you can barely afford to lose to some organisation you detest. Make sure that the money is entrusted with a friend who is instructed to monitor your behaviour and to send off the money the day you fail to spend the amount of time on your project you have contracted to spend.

If you find it particularly difficult to overcome your procrastination – as you might if you have maintained that kind of self-defeating behaviour over a long period of time – try combining rewards with penalties. If you enforce it, this combined assault on your procrastination will normally work. If you won't enforce it, that shows that you are still stubbornly refusing to *work* at changing your ways, and, as we have pointed out repeatedly, if you won't *work* at reducing or eliminating your self-defeating behaviours, then nothing will help you until you do.

In conclusion, if you find yourself slipping back now and then, don't put yourself down for giving in to your procrastinating tendencies. Instead, tackle the main iBs which lie behind your LFT and persist at disputing and eliminating them. Combine one or more of those self-management techniques we outlined above with your disputing techniques and you will improve your chances of at least reducing the frequency and duration of your procrastination.

Finally, distinguish legitimate from illegitimate reasons for delaying carrying out important activities. You may not always get it right, but if you focus on what you are telling yourself at the time about the delay, you will tend to be right more often.

Summary

- *We discussed the barriers that impede effective executive functioning. We drew a distinction between the everyday problems and difficulties that are part and parcel of the life of most executives, and the barriers that are created by the iBs people hold about the circumstances in which they work.*

- *Four principal reasons why people procrastinate were outlined and discussed. The iBs which create and maintain these reasons for procrastinating were identified and rational alternatives were suggested.*

- *We paid particular attention to what we described as the main cause of procrastination, which we identified as Low Frustration Tolerance. We specifically pointed out that LFT would also tend to exacerbate and maintain each of the other reasons why people procrastinate.*

- *We then moved on to consider a number of action techniques which could help one to overcome the problem of procrastination. We described how prioritising one's tasks would help an individual to get started on tackling important tasks which were time-limited. We showed how tying time-tabling to prioritising would help to facilitate the process of steadily working on various tasks and avoid becoming overwhelmed by them.*

- *We outlined two self-management methods of helping to overcome the tendency to procrastinate and showed the advantages of using each of them separately. In cases where procrastination was seen as a particularly difficult problem, we showed how reinforcement and aversive penalties used together could prove more effective.*

6

Taking Anger Out Of The Workplace

Anger- the neglected problem

You may be surprised to learn that anger has received less attention by the psychological community than other emotional problems. It appears that anger is not acknowledged as an emotional problem that people seek treatment for.

Yet, the relatively few serious research studies on anger which have appeared in the psychological literature have shown that anger can be a serious problem for anyone who experiences it. It can not only damage your health, it can damage your relationships with other people, sometimes with tragic consequences. In the workplace, the expression of anger can result in resentment on the part of those on the receiving end, followed frequently by uncooperative behaviour on their part which does nothing for your productivity or office efficiency. These reasons alone, we would suggest, are sufficient justification for encouraging you to take a closer look at this problem of anger and how to control it. Rational-Emotive Training endorses your acknowledging and getting in touch with your feelings. But more importantly it shows you how to distinguish appropriate from inappropriate feelings and how to cultivate the former and at the same time, to reduce or eliminate the latter. But first, let us make clear what we mean by 'anger'. There are no diagnostic categories of anger. Many studies appear every year in the psychological journals on anxiety, or on depression. Plenty of studies can be found which purport to evaluate treatments for anxiety or depression, but anger receives barely a mention. In fact, anger is seen as a problem only when it erupts as violence and causes persistent damage to people or property.

Why has anger been a relatively neglected problem for so long? We suggest that part of the reason is the general perception amongst most people that expressing one's anger is a good thing; it's 'healthy' to let your anger out. Haven't psychologists been telling us in books and articles in newspapers and magazines over several decades now that it is good for us to get in touch with our feelings, to express our emotions, and that it is bad for us to suppress our feelings, especially strong feelings such as anger? And if we refuse to acknowledge our feelings and try to suppress them, they will escape sooner or later and sneak out on us, causing us all sorts of 'embarrassing' predicaments? Yes, we expect you've heard it all before. It is as if our mental energy was governed by the laws of hydraulics: you dam it up here, but soon you find it breaking out there. So you might as well not bother to hold your feelings back. Let them flow! Just let it all 'hang out', was the message of some of the therapies that appeared in the 1960s. Just scream and yell your anger away! As we will show you presently, there are several myths surrounding the subject of anger and the idea that you can get rid of angry, hostile feelings by letting them out, is one of the most widely held of these myths.

What is anger?

English is a language in which some words are used very loosely and cover a range of meanings. 'Anger' is one example. The word is often used indiscriminately and ranges in meaning from mild irritation or annoyance to fury and homicidal rage. So let's be clear about the distinction. Anger is *not* the same kind of feeling as annoyance, even intense annoyance. Each stems from a very different set of beliefs and attitudes as you will see in a moment.

You can tell when you are really angry by anger's physiological effects upon you, and these effects are visible to other people around you. Your blood pressure builds up, you turn red in the face, you tense up, you clench your fists, you tremble as your adrenalin pours into your bloodstream to prepare your whole body for an emergency. It is an uncomfortable feeling and you feel compelled to get rid of it, and that is when you lose control and release your rage by yelling at some-one or acting violently towards him or her. The uncomfortable feeling of tension is dissipated – at least temporarily, but other unfortunate consequences are already in the making. It really isn't in your best interests to live in a violent society, so if you want to help make the world a less violent, happier place to live in, wouldn't you think it worth learning how to diminish hate and anger by becoming a sane, unangry person yourself? And to do so without becoming less assertively driving and goal-directed? You have nothing to lose by trying, and if you are already a person who is prone to displays of anger, the reduced strain on your internal physiological system from learning to live without anger may even add a few years to your life. But first, let's examine the common folk wisdom – the *myths*, which abound on the subject of anger.

Anger- two myths people believe

1. *'Frustration makes me angry'*

Most people today, when faced with the hassles and frustrations of everyday life, assume that they can hardly avoid feeling angry when they are blocked from achieving what they see as their legitimate aims and goals in life. We have no choice, it seems, but to feel angry when others treat us unfairly, cause us considerable inconvenience through their negligence or stupidity, or otherwise interfere with our plans. That seems to be most people's view. It seems also to be the view of quite a few psychologists for the reasons we gave earlier. Anger was not seen as a great problem; there were few studies of anger. The psychologists were probably acquainted with an older well-known viewpoint known as the frustration-aggression hypothesis, which posited the view that frustration makes us angry. So here we had what appeared to be scientific confirmation of what parents, teachers and society had believed all along: being frustrated makes you angry!

If you have come so far with us in your study of this book, you may by now be somewhat sceptical of that proposition – and you would be justified in being so. However, before we explain in detail why your scepticism is justified, let us take a moment to look at the Catch 22 situation people will find themselves in if they believe that certain things can make them feel angry. This leads into Myth No. 2.

2. 'When I'm angry I've only two choices: (a) hold it in, or (b) let it out'

If you believe that, you have virtually no choice at all. Now let us show you why.

Choice No. 1: Hold your anger in!

If you opt for this choice, you bottle up your anger, put the lid on it. Is that healthy, you might ask? Not if you make a habit of it! If you are frequently prone to anger, bottling it up will make you feel like a pressure cooker. Your anger won't dissipate: instead, it will stay right there inside you, ready to break out at any time you relax your control. If you go about seething with suppressed resentment, it won't be long before certain physiological effects begin to manifest themselves. You will develop high blood pressure, you might also experience migraine headaches and stomach ulcers. These are health problems you can certainly do without.

'Well how about my second choice?' you might ask. 'Isn't it supposed to be good and healthy to *let out* our pent up feelings, especially seeing how dangerous to our health it can be to keep them tightly bottled up inside?'

Well, yes, you might avoid the high blood pressure and the migraine attacks. But hadn't you better look at what you might get if you make a habit of expressing your angry feelings, of letting them 'all hang out', as they say?

Choice No. 2: Let your anger out!

We begin by seeing if there are any advantages to expressing one's angry feelings. Then we shall set against these advantages a number of known disadvantages. Once that has been accomplished you will then more clearly appreciate whether or not you have a worthwhile choice between holding your anger in, or letting it out. The advantages of letting your anger out are:

- 'Letting off steam' helps to unbottle your underlying rage and helps it to dissipate. As pointed out above, if you feel angry and do not acknowledge and give vent to your feelings in any way whatever, you stay bottled up and seethe forever – until high blood pressure, etc., gives you other unpleasant things to worry about!

- Anger may be mixed with assertiveness. When anger means largely that you are showing others that you strongly *desire* them to change their behaviour towards you, but that you don't need or have to get them to do so, your anger may denote healthy assertion, rather than puerile 'demandingness' or aggression on your part.

- Releasing hostile feelings can be very pleasurable, especially if you are putting somebody in their place over some alleged fault or misdeed. Releasing angry feelings can also release feelings of depression, although it can also cover up depressed feelings and other feelings you may be loathe to acknowledge.

- Expressing almost any feeling or emotion helps you to learn something about yourself and other people. If you inhibit yourself completely you tend not to learn very much. Even if you do the wrong thing by letting your anger spill out, you can learn from your mistakes and act less mistakenly in future. Severely inhibited individuals waste much of the one life they will ever have because they tragically refuse to experiment with expressing their feelings and thus fail to gain new experiences and become more risk-taking. As a consequence, they miss out on much of what life has to offer them.

• Expressing your anger puts you in touch with some of your important and real feelings. If you habitually bottle up your anger, you tend to refuse to acknowledge that you are displeased, say, with someone's behaviour and that you would very much like him or her to change it. If you express your true feelings you act more authentically and prepare the way to getting at least some of your wants fulfilled.

• Finally, if you frequently let out your angry feelings, you may come to accord them less importance, or reach the stage where you realise you are making a great ado about little or nothing. We're not saying that this will always happen; it usually won't, but occasionally it might!

The disadvantages of letting your anger out are split into two categories: physiological/psychological effects; and interpersonal effects.

Physiological and psychological effects

If you thought that these only occurred to people who habitually held their anger in, you're in for an unpleasant surprise. You've heard of Type A behaviour, right? Well, since Type A behaviour was first identified by Meyer Friedman and Ray Rosenman in 1959, most studies have shown that Type A people are two to three times more at risk from a heart attack than the more relaxed Type B people, but with this important proviso: these Type A individuals who were more at risk were people with an anger problem. Do you know what kind of people are classed as Type A? They are defined as hard-driving, fast-talking, hard-working individuals who are said to be always fighting time or other people. It is important to realise that not all Type A people necessarily have an anger problem. You can be a hard-working, hard-driving individual who abhors waste of time and inefficiency, who keeps subordinates on their toes and who constantly stresses the value of effective time management throughout your organisation, without frequently getting into angry confrontations with others who do not appreciate your views or fail to live up to your own exacting standards.

The classical Type A individual referred to in the literature as 'unusually impatient and *easily roused to hostility*' is obviously an individual with an anger problem. Studies have shown that the Type A behaviour associated with these individuals who also had a problem with anger, predicted cardiovascular problems as well as, or better than any other physiological measure such as high blood pressure, arteriosclerosis, or a serum cholesterol level of 300 or more. Heavy cigarette smoking is also a contributory factor to cardiovascular disease and, according to Friedman, is practically always associated with Type A people. Cigarette smoking may not be quite so frequently associated with Type A people today as it was when Friedman carried out his earlier studies. We know quite a few people we would classify as Type A who are non-smokers. The important point we want to make here is this: the main component of Type A responsible for cardiovascular disease was identified as a free floating hostility. These anger-prone Type A's respond to challenges, especially challenges to their self-esteem, as though they were full scale emergencies. A US government-sponsored study of 800 men who had suffered heart attacks demonstrated that those who had successfully modified their Type A behaviour – that is to say, their propensity to become hostile or enraged, suffered only one-third as many second attacks as those who had only received cardiological counselling.

If you recognise yourself as a Type A person easily roused to anger you could do yourself a big favour by resolving to reduce or eliminate those angry feelings you may be in the habit of expressing. In the following sections we will show you how to go about it. In the meantime, you can accept that being a Type A is no disadvantage in itself; in fact it can confer several major advantages on the individual who is highly motivated to succeed, to achieve peak performance and to reach the top in his or her career. Type A behaviour becomes a problem when the driving force behind it is this free-floating hostility, a readiness to respond angrily to frustrating people or circumstances at the drop of a hat. The important thing to recognise at this point is that whether you hold in your angry feelings or let them out, there is a price to pay in terms of damage to your health.

Interpersonal effects

If damage to one's health were the only disadvantage to expressing anger one had to consider, that would be sufficient reason in itself to make one look for possible alternative strategies for dealing with this destructive emotion. But still other problems have to be faced when other people are involved.

Let's suppose one of your staff is persistently late in getting his monthly report in to you. You have already spoken to him about it, you have stressed how important it is that you receive all reports by a certain time each month so that you can then present your summary report to your chief executive no later than the date he requires it. In spite of your warnings, your subordinate still files his report to you a day later than the deadline you have set. The next time he is late you really tear a strip off him and the entire office hears you. You feel good about expressing your anger, your indignation over the inconvenience he causes you by being late every month with his report.

You feel good, but how do you think he feels when he is on the receiving end of your accusatory and sarcastic words? Your tactics may work in the short term. Nobody enjoys being made to look incompetent or foolish in front of their friends and colleagues. So, your subordinate will give you what you want on time, but grudgingly. Sooner or later he is going to get back at you in some way.

Anger tends to beget anger. You lose cooperation, or it is given resentfully where once it was offered willingly. Your subordinates may fear your wrath and act to protect themselves. But is that going to lead to a highly productive, smooth-running efficient office? We doubt it.

In addition, the expression of anger can be exceptionally time-wasting and side-tracking. It tends to disrupt your personal efficiency by making you preoccupied with your own feelings which in turn distracts you from engaging in more constructive thinking and behaviour. Thus, if you felt annoyed and displeased by your subordinate's chronic lateness but not enraged at *him* you could assertively confront this individual in the privacy of your office and see what explanation, if any, he was able to offer for his persistent failures and then act accordingly. Expressing your anger for its own sake takes over and focuses your attention on the feeling of self-righteous indignation instead of directing your attention to the solution of a problem.

Now, becoming enraged at someone who has committed a blunder may feel good because you feel superior for not having committed a similar blunder, but what happens when you too make a bad mistake that you angrily denigrate others for making? You put yourself down and feel something of a heel. What good will that do you?

All in all, we consider that letting anger out creates more problems than it solves. It may offer a few minor advantages in certain circumstances but the real possibility of damage to your health and to your relations with significant other people in your life outweighs any 'good' things that expressing anger may accomplish.

You may now be wondering: 'If holding my anger in is just not on, and letting it out leads to even worse results, just what the devil am I supposed to do with it?' The good news is that there is a third alternative. It works, and it has no unpleasant consequences. Before we give you the answer that Rational-Emotive Training offers, we want to mention briefly one or two other popular folk remedies for dealing with anger which you have probably heard of, at least, and which are still touted in the media.

Other 'remedies' for anger

Most people feel good about expressing their hostile feelings, or getting it out of their system. But if you let your anger out in front of your boss, or some business client, the consequences can be less than helpful. You lose your client or your boss may fire you.

But suppose that you were given some harmless substitute to express your pent up anger at when you were safely out of sight and sound of people who might take exception if you expressed your angry feelings in their presence; wouldn't that be a good idea? Here are two ways that people have thought up to enable you to 'harmlessly' ventilate your hostility:

The pillow room

This is a technique supposedly favoured by Japanese executives as a way of relieving their angry feelings after a stressful day at the office. The enraged executive is placed in a room by himself with pillows which he pummels and punches while simultaneously imagining he is punching some hated boss or customer. He continues with the punching and name calling until his pent up angry feelings are dissipated or until he becomes exhausted. A variation in the West is to send violent juveniles into a gym and let them kick a ball against the walls of the gym as hard as they like until they get tired of it.

Creative aggression

The idea behind this one – 'constructive anger' it is sometimes called – is that you agree beforehand with the person you feel angry with, to have a session during which each person gives the other 'permission' to vent his or her true feelings about the matter under contention. Presumably this clears the air between the two antagonists and appears to have some merit in that each person is prepared beforehand to listen to the other's angry tirade without feeling surprised or put at a disadvantage by the verbal attacks, as they might in a verbal confrontation that had not been prearranged.

This method is claimed to work best between people who know one another well, such as married couples, family members and other types of close associates. Creative aggression might work well in those cases where the couple concerned can take it, but in other cases it might not work at all. It might even make matters worse because you can never be sure how someone, even someone you know well, will react to a verbal onslaught, especially if the recipient feels very defensive and vulnerable to certain criticisms. The real drawback in our view to this and the preceding technique for dealing with angry feelings is that neither method helps people to really understand how their anger is created in the first place. These methods tacitly assume what most people throughout the world mistakenly believe: that their angry feelings are created by others or frustrating circumstances. The inventors of these and similar techniques also imply that our psychic energy is governed by hydraulic principles and that ways of harm-lessly releasing this energy must be found if an eventual explosion of pent up feeling is to be averted.

We will mention one other method of helping people to deal with their anger before getting down to showing you how your angry feel-ings are really created and how you can eradicate them and lead a calmer existence.

The encounter group

In a therapeutic setting such as this you can express your anger with impunity and even be rewarded by approval from the therapist and other members of the group. If it just stops at merely ventilating your hostility you may feel better and enjoy the approval of those around you for letting your angry feelings out at last. However, unless you are then shown how your anger is created and what you can do to reduce or eliminate it, you are likely to leave the group feeling better, but certainly not *getting* better! For in real life your business associates and your family and friends don't behave like members of an encounter group. Show your boss that you hate him, and you are out of a job or demoted. Tell a neighbour off and you may end up with a feud on your hands. Become enraged at your mate, and you end up with family squabbles which might escalate to the point where divorce is the only answer. Overt anger usually leads to some form of recrimination. If you want to interfere with good relationships, undo good cooperative working arrangements, by all means be as angry as you can and honestly show it!

To *summarise* what we have said so far, we can conclude:

- Holding in your anger is unhealthy, but letting it out is even more unhealthy.

- Neither your working nor your personal life will benefit from the overt expression of anger.

- The use of safe substitutes on which to ventilate your aggression may dissipate your anger in the short term but does not lead to less anger in the long term.

Now, let's see what really goes on in our heads when we become angry and what constructive steps we can take to deal with it.

How you make yourself angry

When accurately defined, anger is a form of demandingness as you will see in a moment. When you are angry with someone, not just very annoyed, but really furious, you tend to damn that person for something he or she has done, or failed to do. Thus, in the example of the subordinate who turned in his monthly reports late each month, we have an example of damning anger directed towards a person.

When you are angry at others the activating event(s), or the inferences you draw about the activating event(s) or 'triggers' as we call them, involve four major themes. These themes centre round situations in which *other people*:

- frustrate you in some way or block you in pursuit of your goals;

- directly attack you or what you value;

- are regarded as threatening you or what you value; and

- transgress your personal rules or code of behaviour.

Thus, when your subordinate continued to hand in his reports late, you were probably telling yourself something like:

1. 'I damned well don't like this man's sloppy behaviour and I wish to hell he would change it!' That's OK. That is a rational statement. If you stayed with that rB you would feel annoyed, and you could express your annoyance at your subordinate's failure to do what you legitimately want him to do and at the fact that you now suffer a certain amount of *frustration* and inconvenience as a result of his inefficient behaviour. That is a provable statement. You are being inconvenienced and you can legitimately feel annoyed and displeased because of the inconvenience and the fact that you are being frustrated in running your department as efficiently as you intend.

   But when you are enraged, not merely annoyed, over your subordinate's unacceptable behaviour, you are adding a highly irrational set of beliefs to your original rational belief. In effect, you are telling yourself:

2. 'Because his failure to send me in his reports on time is frustrating me, he *should not, must not* do it!'

3. 'I find it *awful* to be frustrated.'

4. 'I *can't stand* it!'

5. 'He is a total bastard for treating me like this!'

The iBs listed under (2), (3) and (4) are typical of someone who has a philosophy of Low Frustration Tolerance. Did you recognise them? The fifth iB is the damning component. Did you recognise it as a derivative of major iB No. 2? Here it is highlighted for you in the box:

Major irrational Belief No. 2

Because it is highly desirable that others treat me considerately and fairly, they absolutely should and must do so and they are rotten people who deserve to be utterly condemned when they do not.

Can you see why these four iBs (2) to (5) are untenable? Let us take them in turn.

2. *Because his failure to send me in his reports on time is frustrating me, he should not, must not do it!* This makes no sense because you don't run the universe and it is foolish to command or dictate that because you don't like what someone is doing, therefore he or she must not do it!

3. *I find it awful to be frustrated.* 'Awful' means as bad as bad can be. Is being frustrated really that bad? Frustration is an inconvenience, not a horror.

4. *I can't stand it!* Oh yes, you can! You can tolerate being frustrated without ever liking it.

5. *He is a total bastard for treating me like this!* People who frustrate you are not total bastards but fallible human beings who have their own agendas and will often frustrate you in pursuit of their own goals.

Venting your anger is unhelpful because when you demand, insist, that people do your bidding, you exhibit childish grandiosity. Moreover, your feelings of damning anger will make it more likely that you will verbally abuse your subordinates. If you do this you will hardly enhance your chances of gaining their respect or willing cooperation in achieving your objectives. You may even acquire a reputation amongst your subordinates for being a 'bear with a sore head'. The consequence is often that people will keep their distance from you and grant you only the minimum of help and cooperation. Is that likely to enable you to reach your peak performance or achieve your organisational goals with the minimum of wasted time and effort?

The rational alternative to anger at others

When your goals are blocked you are frustrated. Frustration is a fact, but does frustration *make* you angry? Not if you think clearly. You will feel something, of course, when your desires are blocked, but what you feel is determined largely by how you evaluate what is happening to you. So, imagine you have received yet another late report from your subordinate after you have impressed upon him the importance of getting his reports in on time. As his boss, it is your responsibility to do something about his failure.

Knowing that angering yourself and indignantly taking him to task over his failures isn't going to be the wisest thing you can do, you can, instead, view the matter thus:

- 'I strongly want this man to send me in his reports regularly on time but he doesn't have to.'

- 'I definitely don't like receiving his reports late each month. It is frustrating but it's not calamitous, and I obviously can tolerate it although I'll never like it.'

- 'This fellow is not a louse; he's a fallible human being who's doing the wrong thing. If I have him come in and see what he has to say about it, I can figure out a way of avoiding these delays in future.'

How would you feel if you replaced your irrational damning statements with these more rational ideas? You would feel irritated and displeased by your subordinate's unsatisfactory behaviour and annoyed at being inconvenienced and frustrated by it. Furthermore, you would feel strongly motivated to change the situation. Without in any way damning the man for his inefficient behaviour, you could assertively confront him with the facts and ask him what explanation he had for his chronic late reporting. It may be that he is having legitimate problems in getting his reports out in time, or it may be that he is not all that interested in the job. In either case you can take appropriate action. By focusing on the real problem, you are able to use your management skills to find a solution, but if you let yourself become angry, you tend to get carried away by your upset feeling and lose sight of the real issue. The real problem remains unsolved and you have wasted your own valuable time.

Anger at life conditions

In the previous section we showed that anger at other people is based on a philosophy of LFT, coupled with the iB that whoever frustrates or blocks us is a damnable person. This same basic reason for anger (LFT) is present when one's anger is directed at life conditions instead of at other people. The following example illustrates how anger can emerge when an individual demands that 'Life must be fair!'

Marty worked for a large investment bank. He had been with the bank for many years, had built up a good reputation and was in charge of an entire floor of dealers. Now in his late fifties, Marty was looking forward to early retirement. Marty seldom handled investment assignments himself, preferring to delegate as much as possible and make himself available to dispense his advice and wisdom to anyone whom he thought could do with it.

One morning, Marty's boss came into Marty's office and laid a specially coloured folder on Marty's desk. 'I want you to handle this one yourself, Marty,' said the boss. 'This is a big one and it's important. There's a lot of money involved and we'd better get it right. So don't pass it down the line, Marty. And I'm sorry but you're going to have to work extra hours on this one – late nights and weekends to make sure you catch the various world stock markets when they open.'

As soon as the boss had left Marty's office, Marty thumped his desk and swore under his breath, 'It isn't *fair*! Why did this have to happen to *me*?' Marty's basic iB was: 'Life *must* go smoothly and pleasantly for me, especially now when I'm getting ready to retire!' From this iB, Marty concluded the following:

- 'It's *unfair* that I've been given this assignment and that shouldn't happen!'

- 'It's *terrible* that I'm going to have to work long unsocial hours!'

- 'I *can't stand* having all this extra hassle just when I'm planning to take things easy with my retirement coming up!'

- 'The world's a *rotten* place when things like this can happen!'

Do you recognise major iB No. 3?

Major irrational Belief No. 3

Because it is preferable that I experience pleasure rather than pain, the world absolutely should arrange this and life is horrible, and I can't bear it when the world doesn't.

Since we have already disputed this major iB in the previous section and in other chapters there is no need to repeat ourselves. We suggest you help yourself to raise your level of frustration tolerance by developing a rational philosophy towards frustration. Check back to the appropriate chapters if you want some reminders of why this major iB is irrational and see if the rational alternative philosophy you come up with looks like this:

- 'I would like things to tick over smoothly for me until I retire but they probably won't and they don't have to.'

- 'It's a pain in the neck that this important job has come in and will entail me working nights and weekends but it's hardly *awful* or *terrible!*'

- 'I can certainly tolerate it and if I have to delay slightly my plans to retire, that's just too bad. I won't like it but I can stand it.'

- 'Just because I'm being inconvenienced at a time when I least want it hardly proves that the world is a rotten place. Let's face it, the world is a complex mix of good, bad and neutral. Tough! That's the way it is.'

In the above example, Marty was not angry with his boss. He realised that his boss had no option but to assign the job to the most experienced member of his staff. However, just for argument's sake, imagine yourself in Marty's position and that you really are angry with your boss for having given you the special assignment.

You had better not denounce your boss for allegedly treating you unfairly! So, after you have studied the previous section and agreed that it is unhelpful to damn others for frustrating you, let's offer you an additional strategy for nipping your anger in the bud before it can do you any harm.

Using Rational-Emotive Imagery (REI)

This is a technique you can use to prepare yourself in advance for an encounter you think might trigger in you an angry reaction. Unlike other emotional upsets like anxiety or depression where you have plenty of time to tackle the iBs which underlie them, in the case of anger you don't get much time to identify your iBs and marshal your rational alternatives.

Rational-Emotive Imagery in effect buys you time. What you do is to imagine as vividly as you can a situation wherein your boss calls you in and gives you a lot of extra work and responsibility. Imagine yourself feeling really angry at having all this put on you. Really get in touch with your anger. Feel yourself getting enraged.

When you have done that, repeat the same scene in your mind, but this time force yourself to feel annoyed and very displeased instead of hostile or enraged. When you have succeeded in doing that, identifying the beliefs you used to change your anger to annoyance and displeasure.

Your rBs probably were along the lines of:

- 'Here I am being given this extra work he promised me. I don't like being given more work because I think I'm doing enough already. However, he doesn't have to do what I want him to do.'

- 'As the boss, he has the right to decide who does what around here, and while I don't enjoy having to work late nights or weekends I can clearly stand it.'

If you practise this imagery technique several times a day before your encounter with your boss, you will be much better prepared to respond in a manner which will help you achieve your objectives than if you allow yourself to angrily blow your top or hold your anger inside and seethe with suppressed indignation at the alleged 'unfairness' and 'horror' at being selected to take on the extra work load.

If you take the assertive option

In the example we gave you of anger directed at life conditions, it was clear that Marty had no quarrel with his boss over being given the assignment and the extra work that would be involved, but rather with what Marty perceived as the unfairness of life conditions as they affected him.

However, there may well be circumstances where you have grounds for thinking that you have been unfairly singled out to take on extra work or responsibilities without any mention of extra remuneration whatever. If you consider you have a case and decide to assertively confront your boss over your work load and ask him for some acceptable rearrangement of the work, there are a few points to bear in mind:

- First, get his attention. Make sure it is a good time and that he is able to devote a few minutes to hear you out.

- Describe the problem objectively. Explain what you have difficulty with and why. Don't attribute motives to your boss. Watch your inferences and evaluations! Don't use interpretative statements, be factual.

- Listen carefully to his response and then make a suitable response in reply. Look upon it as a mutual problem to be solved rather than an argument to be won.

- Communicate only information relevant to the matter under discussion. Omit feelings! Focus only on the facts – time, costs, advantages/disadvantages of doing it his way compared with your alternative suggestions.

- Know your boss! Does he compromise when presented with a reasonable alternative? Or does he always get his own way? Remember that you can be really nice and politely assertive but still be fired if your boss refuses to go along with your ideas! So think carefully before you assert yourself.

We will now take a detailed look at one more kind of anger which it is important to be aware of.

Ego defensive anger

This is the kind of anger an individual may experience in an encounter where the individual infers that the actions or responses of other people transgress a personal rule decreed important by that individual. The transgression of this personal rule is interpreted as a threat to the rule-holder's 'self-esteem'. Perhaps we can make clear what we mean by the following example.

Using anger to protect one's self-worth

Amanda and Jeff worked for a firm of magazine publishers. Both began their career with the firm at the same time. Amanda was eager to learn the ins and outs of the entire business, and being a bright and intelligent person, she worked diligently to achieve her objectives. Unfortunately, Amanda had always attached her self-worth to achievement. As a child she was taught that she didn't amount to much unless she did extremely well at whatever she was given to do. Amanda's father did not hide his disappointment when Amanda was born. He had never wanted a daughter; having only male children was what he wanted. In his view females were a kind of lesser breed and were to be treated accordingly.

When Amanda eventually was promoted to the management team of the publishing firm it was generally agreed that she had won her appointment on merit and that her promotion was thoroughly deserved. For Amanda, her appointment proved that she was at last worthy of respect. In her eyes, promotion to management validated her self-worth. 'At long last,' thought Amanda, 'I am somebody, and no longer just a nobody!'

Amanda let it be known that now that she had reached management team status, she wished to be addressed by members of the staff by her surname preceded by 'Ms'. No longer would she be 'Amanda' to her friends and colleagues, but 'Ms Dorman'. Jeff, for his part, was delighted to hear of Amanda's appointment, and although he was careful to use the formal mode of address requested by Amanda when communicating with her officially, he saw no reason to do so when they happened to meet off duty in the staff restaurant where Jeff – and one or two other old colleagues of Amanda's – would greet her as 'Amanda'.

Amanda made herself furiously angry whenever anyone, and Jeff in particular, used her first name. Amanda regarded others' attempts to remain on first name terms with her as evidence of lack of respect for her. Moreover, she inferred that Jeff and one or two others were secretly jealous of her for winning promotion and probably resented her for it because she was a female.

Amanda made herself angry because of her implicit iB: 'I *must* be treated with respect by everybody on the staff, bar none! And if people show that they don't respect me that proves that I am unworthy of respect and am basically worthless.' From this basic iB Amanda then drew the following irrational conclusions:

- 'It's *terrible* that some members on the staff don't show me the respect that they should.'

- 'I *can't bear it* when they show that they do not respect me.'

- 'They are *rotten*, women-downing people for treating me disrespectfully and for reminding me of my basic worthlessness.'

Amanda's primary problem was not her anger but her low sense of self-worth. Her anger served to protect her from her basic feelings of worthlessness which she experienced whenever anyone said or did anything which reminded her of it.

To help Amanda to acquire self-acceptance she would first be shown how to overcome her anger at her subordinates' presumed lack of respect for her. She would accomplish this by replacing her previous anger-creating demands with these more rational beliefs:

- 'I want to be treated with respect by the staff but they don't have to obey my rule. It's unfortunate if they appear to disrespect me but I can accept myself as a fallible human being whether or not these others respect me, and whether or not I continue to hold my management position.

- 'It's bad but not terrible when Jeff and the others don't treat me always as I want them to.'

- 'I can jolly well stand their disrespectful behaviour although I might never like it.'

- 'Neither Jeff nor any of my previous colleagues are rotten people for not treating me at all times as I want them to. They are fallible, unrateable human beings who are not doing as I desire. Too bad!'

Once Amanda acquired this set of rational beliefs she would be in a much better position to question the validity of her inferences that Jeff and certain others called her by her first name because they were jealous of her. Even if she were right about some of her colleagues being jealous and resentful of her success, that might merely indicate that they had a problem, but that there was no reason why Amanda should make it her problem. In any event, Amanda's attitude of non-damning acceptance of her colleagues would encourage her to try to influence them in some constructive way to always address her by her surname if she still thought this desirable. By contrast, Amanda's feelings of damning anger would decrease her chances of having good respectful relationships with her colleagues in the future.

Finally, once Amanda were to truly abandon her childhood-acquired iB that she could only accept herself as having worth when she did outstandingly well, and instead could unconditionally accept herself as having intrinsic value to herself regardless of whether or not she achieved great things in life, she could question the necessity of sticking rigidly to her rule that colleagues must address her formally at all times. With her new philosophy that she needed no external symbols to validate herself as a human with intrinsic value to herself, Amanda could then afford to relax her rule in the knowledge that if her colleagues wished to address her informally in appropriate circumstances, that did not necessarily imply lack of respect for her on their part.

Summary

- *We began by distinguishing anger from annoyance and described the uncomfortable physiological effects which accompany anger and clearly distinguish it from annoyance.*

- *Two myths people believe about anger were discussed. The first myth, 'frustration makes me angry' is almost universally accepted as true as is the second myth that when you are angry, you have only two options: 'Hold it in!' or 'Let it out!'*

- *We listed the unhealthy consequences of holding in one's angry feelings and then considered in some detail the relative advantages and disadvantages of letting one's anger out. We showed that while expressing anger possessed a few advantages of limited value, the disadvantages outweighed the advantages and could have serious health consequences for the individual who habitually expressed enraged feelings.*

- *After a discussion of Type A behaviour (which is fairly common amongst executives) and its relationship with anger, we concluded that studies supported our view that Type A behaviour itself did not predict health problems but the anger component sometimes associated with Type A behaviour predicted these problems.*

- *In addition to its dangerous physiological effects we went on to show that the open expression of anger frequently soured or disrupted interpersonal relationships. We argued that the expression of anger can be exceptionally time-wasting and side-tracking and that overall, expressing anger created more problems than it solved.*

- *We then went on to consider some popular strategies for dealing with anger. We identified their good points as well as their limitations, and showed that none of them effectively addressed the real cause of anger and how to eliminate it.*

- *When accurately defined, anger is a form of demandingness and we showed how one makes oneself angry (a) at other people and (b) at the world or life conditions as a result of holding specific iBs which lead to anger-creating philosophies.*

- *Ways of eliminating some common forms of anger through replacing the relevant iBs with rational alternatives were explained by means of appropriate examples. We also offered Rational-Emotive Imagery (REI) as a useful additional technique one could profitably use whenever an angry confrontation is anticipated.*

- *We drew your attention to a number of points to bear in mind should you decide to assertively confront someone over you in a matter involving disagreement over work practices, for example.*

- *Finally, we considered ego-defensive anger, a type of anger that is directed at others whom we incorrectly think are threatening our 'self-esteem'. We showed how to overcome ego-defensive anger by challenging the iBs that underpin it. In particular we showed that a person's self-worth is not dependent on how he or she is treated by others or whether he or she performs outstanding deeds.*

7

Become A Workaphile Not A Workaholic

Since the purpose of definitions is to include all that is covered by the definition but also to exclude all that is not covered, we will begin by defining what we understand and mean by the term, 'workaholic'.

In her book, *Workaholics: Living with them, working with them* (New American Library, 1980) Marilyn Machlowitz includes many interesting observations derived from fascinating interviews with scores of individuals she termed workaholics. Were these individuals best described as 'workaholics'? Here are some typical descriptions: intense, goal-driven, sleeps only a minimum number of hours each night, a 16-hour working day, vacations or time off practically non-existent. They never have enough time, they are never bored. No matter how much they have accomplished, it is never enough. There's always something more or greater to accomplish. And they don't need any 'thank you's' or expressions of appreciation. Give them a goal, something not too easy to achieve, something to get really excited about- so long as they are totally absorbed in something big, ongoing, creative, challenging, they are content to go on and on. Workaholics don't retire. For them, retirement is death.

So far so good. Without necessarily being definitive, these descriptions seemed to fit many workaholics, but not all. In her study of workaholics in the book referred to above, Marilyn Machlowitz observed that some of those she interviewed were unhappy to be classed as workaholics. For some, the word 'workaholic' carried negative overtones because of its connection with 'alcoholic'. Apparently 'workaholism' owes its origin to 'alcoholism' and this naturally conveyed the negative image of an addiction. We realised of course that some workaholics could be addicted to work. You can become addicted to virtually anything. And not everyone considers that workaholics are models to be emulated. The workaholic is sometimes seen as the victim of some sort of social disease, someone who is driven by anxiety or a deep sense of insecurity to immerse himself in work, to become a slave to a very demanding set schedule, and thus achieve some degree of escape from his inner fears.

Workaphile or workaholic?

We've all heard of stress. A few years ago, Hans Selye pointed out that there are two kinds of stress – good stress which he termed 'eustress', and bad stress which he termed 'distress'. In a similar vein we believe there are two kinds of workaholism: compulsive and non-compulsive.

Compulsive workaholics – whom we shall refer to henceforth in this chapter as *workaholics* – work practically all the time because of their absolutist commands or demands upon themselves. They cling to certain iBs about their activities. For example they tell themselves and strongly believe: 'I *must* work and achieve to prove I am a worthwhile person!'; or if they feel upset about not working all the time they believe 'I *have* to keep working, working to protect myself from idleness because I *can't stand* being idle for a single minute because it leads me to constant worrying!'

As a result of their believing in these irrational *needs*, these workaholics desperately drive themselves to keep working, working all the time. However, not everyone who makes work the major part of their life is compulsively driven to work.

The non-compulsive workaholic

Unlike the compulsively driven workaholic, this other kind of highly work-oriented individual – the non-compulsive workaholic who we shall henceforth denote by the term, *workaphile* – does not use work as a defence against anxiety or emotional involvement, but works because he or she actively *enjoys* working and the results that come from it. This second kind of healthy workaholic – the *workaphile* – strongly *prefers* effort to idleness or relaxation, but can be quite happy without it, though less happy than when actively engaged in meaningful work. Workaphiles enjoy working but they can also enjoy themselves in many other ways such as participation in sports, games, music, art, literature and other non-working involvements and entertainments.

Some workaphiles are outstanding performers in their particular fields mainly because they genuinely like doing what they do more than they like anything else in the world. Assuming that you are dedicated to achieving peak performance in your chosen field of activity and strongly desire to reach your personal and organisational objectives with the minimum of waste of time, how would you become a workaphile rather than a workaholic? As already hinted at, the central issue is your attitude to work, your core beliefs about work and the meaning you give to work and to life itself. One of Freud's sanest observations was that virtually all of us are driven by two main impulses: work and love. We would agree in the main with that but would add one important modification: the essence of work is not labour but is goal-seeking and action. For the true workaphile, Work spelt with a capital W means some vital absorbing interest- some large long-range project which is seen as vitally important, something worth doing for its own sake with or without financial reward, something the workaphile really *wants* to do and would find it almost impossible not to get involved in. Not so much work *and* love, as Freud put it, but a kind of unified process of work-love.

This doesn't mean that the workaphile's other life enjoyments are severely limited or even non-existent. Far from it! The rationally-motivated workaphile is seldom without a wide range of enjoyable or

149

interesting vocations to pursue. The main drawback is lack of time to pursue them all! He or she is no one-dimensional type of person but an individual who is highly motivated to make this one life as rewarding and fulfilling as is possible within the existing constraints of time and circumstance. He or she will usually be devoted to one major involvement which may mean a lifetime of commitment to that particular project, but will also tend to pursue and value other non-working kinds of commitments.

Are you a workaholic?

If you suspect that you may be a workaholic, or even a potential workaholic, you might like to ask yourself the following questions. We will then go on to take a more detailed look at the iBs which underlie workaholism, two of which we touched on in the previous section. Now here are the questions:

- Do you feel driven to work because so long as you are working you are not bored but become bored very quickly when you stop working so that you can't focus on any non-work activity?

- Do you feel distinctly upset or edgy when you are not working or are prevented from working by some external circumstance?

- Do you believe that you have to engage in work even though you don't enjoy it just because it is *work*?

- Is there a compulsive quality about your involvement in your work? Do you feel like an addict who has no choice but to work and work compulsively and frantically?

If you can answer 'yes' to any of these questions the chances are that you are a workaholic or near to becoming one! If you want to stay that way and are willing to accept the consequences, fine. There's nothing we can do except to advise you to accept that you are a workaholic but that you don't have to condemn yourself for being a workaholic.

On the other hand, if you feel you would do much better and possibly be a lot happier by surrendering your compulsive workaholism and replacing it with the alternative healthy non-compulsive 'workaholism' – become a workaphile in other words – then go on to the next section. There we will show you how to distinguish the workaphile from the workaholic and how to become a workaphile if you want to.

The irrational Beliefs of workaholics

The following iBs are typical of those stoutly adhered to by compulsive workaholics.

- *'I **have** to keep working, working all the time at this particular business and be outstandingly successful to prove I am worth while!'*

  How does working and becoming a great success prove you are worth while? All it would prove is that hard work can sometimes (not necessarily always!) bring success. And where is it written that you absolutely have to be outstandingly successful? Achievement by itself says nothing about your intrinsic worth to yourself unless you arbitrarily define it so. The belief that you have no worth unless you have accomplished is irrational as is the equally silly belief that because you have accomplished, you then have value as a person.

- *'It's **awful** not to work because I get bored then and I **can't stand** being bored.'*

  Is being bored really the worst possible thing that could happen to you? Granted you find it unpleasant and frustrating but where is the evidence that you can't stand it? You can stand virtually anything until you physically collapse! And why can't you creatively use your boredom to motivate you to experiment open-mindedly with engaging in non-work-related activities to determine how much you enjoy these?

- *'I'll **have** to keep working, working for the rest of my life and I can never stop and relax or enjoy myself.'*

That sounds as if you were made specially to work and that you are incapable of doing anything else. Who says you have to work or do anything, for that matter? Until you try something different how do you know you can never stop working?

As you can see, all these iBs are built on some form of absolutism. They cannot be proved, they are unrealistic and illogical and will almost always lead to poor results. When you feel compulsively driven to do anything, you are in a trap, and no longer a free agent for you see yourself as having no choice. Once you challenge these iBs you will see that you almost always do have some choice as to what you can do with your life.

Rational alternatives to the Beliefs of workaholics

- *'I prefer to keep working in this particular business but I don't have to. I want to be successful and if I am, that will be rewarding. But if I am not successful, that is unfortunate, but I can accept myself as a fallible human being with worth to myself whether or not I achieve outstandingly.'*

With this rB you would work in your chosen business because you wanted to, not because you felt you had to. You would feel free to strive for a successful outcome to your work but you would not feel terribly upset if you failed, nor would you condemn yourself as worthless or a total failure if a successful outcome eluded you.

- *'I may get bored for a time when I'm not working or unable to work, but being bored is an inconvenience and not working is frustrating, but I can stand it even although I'll never like being idle.'*

By refusing to upset yourself when you are temporarily idle you can accept the boredom and frustration as inevitable but not awful and motivate yourself to find some interest or activity to see you through the waiting period until you can resume work once more.

- *'I would like to keep working for the rest of my life because I find it intrinsically enjoyable, but I don't have to do so. There is no reason why I can't allow myself some relaxation and enjoy myself in other suitable ways.'*

Once you get rid of the compulsive element you can devote yourself to working at some long-range goal for the rest of your life if you want to without necessarily shutting yourself off from several other enjoyable pursuits and interests.

Now let's look at the situation of the dedicated workaphile. What problems might he or she encounter in relation to significant others such as a spouse or parents or children in the course of the workaphile's working life?

Can being a workaphile get you into trouble?

The short answer is, yes it can in certain circumstances; for example, if the spouse or family members are not workaphiles themselves and have a great deal of time on their hands or when they are very 'needy' of love. In these circumstances workaphiles would be wise to accept that they don't have to do as much work as they do and that it might be wiser for them to spend more time with their loved ones or somehow compensate these loved ones in other ways. One recommended solution is that the workaphile mate only with another workaphile, and then they are both busy and don't push each other to stop working.

Another practical solution that sometimes works is for the workaphile to give the partner who complains about his or her working too much, a decent amount of *quality* time and do exactly what the partner would like in that time whatever that may be, but not to spend too much time at it.

You can sometimes compensate the deprived partner in other ways such as to give him or her more money or more sex or whatever else they might like for compensation.

Another solution is to show the deprived partner or child that he or she really doesn't *need* extra time although that might be quite desirable. In other words, the workaphile can to some degree use RET to help the deprived one stop his or her complaining and just feel sorry and disappointed rather than horrified about being deprived.

What if workaholism is still a problem?

In a previous section we drew your attention to the main iBs which drive people into workaholism and then showed how to replace these iBs with appropriate rational alternative Beliefs. However, as we have stated a number of times throughout this book, merely understanding and agreeing with the. rational ideas we have presented will not usually be sufficient by itself to enable you to undo a long-established dysfunctional habit such as workaholism can become. Achieving intellectual insight into the irrational underpinnings of compulsive behaviours or addictions is only the first step. You will find that only by practising disputing in a vigorous manner the basic iBs which underpin your addiction – whether it be to work or anything else – and by acting persistently against those iBs and feelings which sustain it, will you weaken their influence sufficiently to enable you to replace them with healthier ways of behaving. In the following sections we will provide you with a comprehensive battery of emotive and behavioural techniques with which you can augment and strengthen your disputing skills to enable you to truly uproot those tenacious iBs and attitudes which may still be holding you a captive of workaholism and preventing the emergence of a healthy workaphilism.

Combating workaholism: cognitive emotional and behavioural methods

Cognitive methods

We could call this, 'the irrational Beliefs of workaholics revisited'. Cognitive methods are simply thinking methods. Their main aim is to encourage you to reason things out; you look for evidence of the truth or falsity of various Beliefs. Are the Beliefs logical? Do they make sense? Are they likely to help you reach your goals? Or are they doing the opposite? These are the questions you ask yourself. Now return to the section headed 'The irrational Beliefs of workaholics'. Study carefully the iBs which we identified there as the basic iBs underlying workaholism. Virtually what they are all saying is: 'I *have* to work, and it will be *awful* if I don't!' If you have come with us so far, you will readily agree that so far as human beings are concerned, there are no 'have to's' or 'got to's' in the universe. Maybe the earth and its sister planets have to revolve round the sun because that is the law of the universe, a law of celestial mechanics; but humans almost always have a choice of what to think and do within the limits set by their biology. We don't have total freedom but neither are we robots programmed from birth to behave only in fixed ways, although some workaholics might give one that impression!

So, once you have convinced yourself that these iBs underlying workaholism are indeed irrational, that they cannot rationally be upheld, you can still further promote your efforts to undo them and to replace them with more rational convictions by the use of *coping statements*. These are rational self-statements which you repeat to yourself in a forceful manner over and over again until the rational message contained in these statements really sinks in. In terms of our present discussion a typical coping statement would be: 'I prefer very much to work a great deal of the time but I *don't have to*. I can lead a good or better life not working that much.'

Referenting

Referenting is another technique you can use. In referenting you make a list of the advantages and disadvantages of compulsive working and then choose whether or not to change. In the case of workaholism, some fairly typical disadvantages would be:

- Deterioration in your relationships with your spouse and/or children. If you compulsively work long hours and take very little time off, your loved ones may complain that they see you only at weekends, and sometimes not even then. If you have young children and spend a great deal of time away from them, they may grow up through their more formative years without ever having got to know you as a parent. To them you become a stranger.

- Your health may be impaired to the extent that your physician may order you to rest or take a long vacation on pain of suffering serious cardiovascular problems in the future.

- You may be allowing yourself so little social life that friends you previously saw and spent time with will conclude that you no longer are interested in maintaining a relationship with them, and slowly drift out of your life.

Using Rational-Emotive Training with others

You could use the principal teachings of Rational-Emotive Training set out in this book and try to talk other people out of *their* workaholism, and show them the disadvantages of it. In teaching RET to others you will tend to strengthen your own rational convictions by learning how to counter their objections and thus learn to 'think on your feet' when confronted by your own iBs. But a word of advice! Don't play the role of unwanted counsellor to your workaholic colleagues unless they show some interest in what you have learned from RET and are willing to discuss it with you.

Psychoeducational methods might also appeal to you. You could read RET books, listen to RET tapes, or attend RET workshops where you could learn many practical ways of dealing with all kinds of emotional problems, including workaholism.

Imaging

You can use imaging by imagining yourself not working all the time and feeling disappointed, but determined to enjoy yourself in other ways. If you rehearse this frequently you will help yourself to build a bridge between intellectually understanding rational concepts and really becoming convinced of them and feeling comfortable when carrying them out in practice.

Reframing

In reframing you look for the benefits you can gain from non-work activities which you had previously dismissed as a waste of good working time. You could look into such activities as sports and recreations. You could pick up some sport you had previously enjoyed, such as basketball or tennis, and find out how much you still enjoy playing it. Or you could try various other recreational pursuits including some you had never previously considered and find out by engaging in them what really gives you pleasure and enjoyment. Discover, through thinking, experimenting and risk-taking what you personally find pleasurable and enjoyable so that you no longer see your work as your only possible source of satisfaction in life.

Cognitive distraction

These techniques could be worth trying. By relaxing through medita-tion or yoga or other techniques you could interrupt the constant barrage of workaholic messages flowing through your brain and give yourself leeway to get away from seeing working as an absolute necessity.

Modelling

Modelling yourself on someone who is not a workaholic could be useful, especially if he or she was actually a confirmed workaphile! Find out how this person does it. What does this person believe about work? How does he or she see work in relation to other aspects of life? What is this person's philosophy of life? Discover if you can what kind of daily regime he or she follows and see if you can adapt it to your own particular circumstances.

Problem solving

This is a skill possessed by most executives. You can use your prob-lem-solving abilities and executive talent to do all your work in less time, thereby giving yourself more time to undertake or try out non-work activities such as sport, in order to help yourself to break the workaholic habit. The more efficient you have become at doing your job, the better able you should be at making time to experiment with and develop non-work interests, and thus break your workaholic habit.

Adopting a philosophy of self-acceptance and fallibility

This is an excellent aid to resolve problems with workaholism. Nobody is perfect and you will never be perfect no matter how hard you work. Accept yourself as a fallible human being who doesn't have to prove worth by outstanding achievement. Your worth to yourself is not on the line and is independent of your achievements. Strive to *do* your best, rather than *be* the best. Achieve – not for the sake of achieving, not to receive adoration from others, not to prove your greatness as a person – but just for the plain enjoyment of achieving.

A vital absorbing interest

A vital absorbing interest in some recreational pursuit, such as music, art or sport is yet another way of taking yourself away from your work and thoughts of work. Becoming involved in something which really holds your interest other than work is recommended as a useful diversionary method for taking your mind off work or obsessively thinking of work.

Semantic

Semantic methods are useful in clarifying the way you think. To do this you change your language. Instead of saying to yourself, 'I *should* or *must* keep working,' you can change that to, 'It is preferable to keep working, but it is also preferable to do other things.' Or, instead of saying: 'Doing great work or hard work makes me a great person!', you could say: 'I *think* doing great work or hard work makes me a great person but it actually doesn't.' Or again, instead of saying: 'I can't change and stop being a workaholic!', you can say: 'I find it difficult but I *can* change.'

Changing your language can help a little to diminish an obsessive 'need' to be always working, but unless your more rational language leads to or reflects a deep philosophic change in your attitude towards work, the effect on your workaholism will tend to be slight and probably short-lived. However, if you tie in with your semantic efforts a determined and vigorous attack on your iBs which underlie your workaholism, you will find this double-barrelled assault on your workaholism more effective.

Emotive methods

Under this heading we include several techniques which are designed to promote emotional insight. These techniques encourage you to feel differently about some problem, not just by imagining yourself doing something difficult or 'scary' but actually doing it.

Rational-Emotive Imagery

We have already introduced you to REI in Chapter 6 so we need not go over it again in detail. In the context of workaholism you would proceed by imagining yourself lolling around enjoying recreational things or just doing nothing and then letting yourself feel very anxious and upset if that is what you would be likely to feel. Then you change your feelings of anxiety or panic to sorrow or disappointment or even happiness that you were able to enjoy such activities. You would then carefully note what you told yourself to change your feelings of anxiety or panic to sorrow, etc., and practise these new self-statements until you felt comfortable imagining yourself enjoying non-work activities.

Shame-attacking exercises

This type of exercise can be another useful way of pushing yourself into doing something you are irrationally afraid of doing or being seen to do. You can go out of your way to tell people that you are a workaholic and that you have a tendency to compulsively work but not feel ashamed about it. Or you could do recreational things which you would normally be ashamed to do but force yourself not to feel ashamed. If you do feel ashamed, revise the techniques we showed you in an earlier chapter (Chapter 3) on how to combat feelings of shame and embarrassment. Let us briefly remind you again: When you feel ashamed you negatively evaluate your *self* for acting in a way in which you and/or others consider weak, foolish or inadequate. The main iB you would tackle is the Belief that acting stupidly or inadequately makes you a stupid or inadequate person. When you denigrate yourself, you are equating yourself with your actions. You will recall that we have been at pains to point out several times in this book that you are not the same thing as your behaviour. Once you accept that, you will tend to feel regret, but not shame, over your allegedly inadequate behaviour, and feel able to re-evaluate your behaviour in the light of your more rational Beliefs.

Forceful coping statements

These consist of very vigorously telling yourself that 'I don't *have* to keep working all the time and I can lead quite a good life and accept myself without doing the work.' You could put your irrational ideas about workaholism on a three or four minute tape and then *vigorously* dispute these ideas and listen to it and get your friends, relatives or your Rational-Emotive trainer to listen to it.

Role-playing

This can be done with a friend, with you playing the role of a person enjoying himself or herself by not working all the time and trying to persuade your opposite number who plays a workaholic to agree with your ideas. This exercise should be tape-recorded. If anxiety is experienced during the role-playing, the tape is stopped, and you find out what you are feeling anxious about and identify and dispute the iBs behind the anxiety until it disappears.

Use catchy sayings

You can often convey a rational message to yourself through the use of a pithy comment or catchy phrase or saying. For example, if you think that not working all the hours of the day is about the worst thing that could happen to you, you could repeat to yourself several times: 'From the day you're born, until you ride in the hearse, there's nothing so bad that it couldn't be worse.' You could remind yourself of that saying by printing it on a small card and reading it out loud to yourself several times a day.

Behavioural methods

We have stressed throughout this book that thinking, feeling and behaving are all inter-related; and we have emphasised that if you wish to effect a deep philosophic change at either the specific or general level towards a more rational view of life, you had better employ a battery of methods designed to encourage not only more rational ways of thinking, but also more appropriate ways of feeling and behaving. In previous sections we have outlined well-tried cognitive and emotive techniques to help you achieve that goal. We now invite you to consider a few behavioural methods designed to reinforce those other methods and harden your new rational outlook.

'In-vivo desensitisation'

This is one method commonly used. It involves forcing yourself to engage in recreational activities or just relaxing and doing virtually nothing until you get used to it. You can deliberately stay with a group of non-workaholics or people who are only interested in pleasure and not upset yourself about it and then decide if you can accept some of these pleasures yourself.

Since workaholics tend to fear and shun long periods of idleness, this type of desensitisation confronts the workaholic 'head on' with a challenge to his or her most basic fears. If coupled with simultaneous cognitive disputing, the technique can be quite effective in making inroads into compulsive behaviours such as workaholism.

Form a relationship or join a group

You could get into a deep relationship with a person who is not a workaholic and use that relationship so well that you would be willing to give up some of your workaholism for the relationship. Following on from the theme of the paragraph above, by joining a group of people who regularly go in for recreation rather than workaholism and through becoming attached to that group, you could acquire a different perspective on life and become less strongly attached to your workaholism.

Self-management methods

You could reward yourself for engaging in recreation and non-work activities and penalise yourself when you insist on being too workaholic. Follow the procedures outlined on pages 118-119 in the sections headed 'Contingency management' and 'The use of penalties'.

Skill training

You could help yourself combat your workaholism by getting skill training in some kind of sport or recreational activity such as music or art or other things such as social skills training which would take you away from your workaholism.

All told therefore, you could employ quite an array of cognitive, emotive and behavioural techniques to help you give up your workaholism. By combining various methods from each modality – cognitive plus emotive plus behavioural – simultaneously, and employing them persistently and vigorously, you could substantially change your compulsion to work, work, work, in a remarkably short space of time. However, there is something else you need if you wish to become a workaphile and to remain a workaphile for most of your life; you need good health!

Follow a rigorous health regime

Assuming you have a reasonably good family history for good health and suffer from no serious problems at the moment, you would be wise to adopt a fairly rigorous health regime. There are plenty of good books and videos available now so we need not duplicate the advice they offer. Find a diet and exercise regime that suits you and stick to it. If you already have a health programme, review it and decide if anything in it needs changing to ensure that it is fulfilling the demands made upon you by your particular life-style.

By following common sense rules of health and physical relaxation and by using the principles of Rational-Emotive Training on yourself, you can nicely conserve your energies and enjoy both your work and your recreational pursuits for maybe a period of many years. We wish you success, but to give you that extra cutting edge to your determination to become a happy, long-life workaphile, we suggest you carefully read the following section. You have already come a fair way towards acquiring a rational philosophy of life if you have read and conscientiously applied the advice we have offered you in this book. However, it is one thing to feel you have acquired a rational outlook; it is another thing to maintain it! As you go along, you will experience occasions when your rational philosophy will be severely tested. In view of the subject matter of this chapter, and the fact that we espouse workaphilism as consistently as we can, it seemed appropriate to recommend you to apply your workaphilism to the Rational-Emotive Training you have been working hard at acquiring ever since you began your reading of this book. Hence the title of the penultimate section of this chapter, which seems to us also a fitting way to end this book.

Become a workaphile at Rational-Emotive Training

How will you feel when, after a period of progress in using Rational-Emotive Training to overcome various self-defeating thoughts, feelings and behaviours and feeling much more confident about your ability to react rationally and to deal adequately with all kinds of difficult people or circumstances, you fall back sometimes far back? If your reaction is similar to many people who have benefited from applying RET principles to their lives, but have subsequently slipped back, you will tend to put yourself down for having allowed an old problem to arise and smite you again. Perhaps you feel ashamed at having displayed weakness in allowing some previously solved problem to recur and get the better of you again. Let's say you had a confrontation with someone in your office, and instead of dealing firmly and calmly with the other person, you 'lost your cool' and ended up in an angry shouting match.

You felt angry but soon afterwards you felt ashamed of yourself for having become enraged. You then had two problems for the price of one! You probably told yourself: 'What an idiot I am for having lost my temper with so-and-so last week. After all I've learned from Rational-Emotive Training I *ought* to have known better!'

Remember that no one is perfect and practically all of us take one step backwards for every two steps forwards. Why? Because that is the nature of we humans: we improve, we stop improving at times, and sometimes we backslide. So, how can you slow down your tendency to fall back? Here are some methods that we have tested and have used personally and which many of our clients have found quite effective.

How to maintain your gains

1. When you fall back to old feelings of anger, depression or self-denigrating, remind yourself and pinpoint exactly what thoughts, feelings and behaviours you once changed to bring about your improvement. For example, if you feel ashamed at losing your temper in the office, recall how you challenged the irrational idea that you were a no-good person because you acted badly or inappropriately. Go back and rehearse the arguments you went through to convince yourself that a mistaken or

wrong act does not make you a bad person. Remember and apply the important principle of refraining from rating your *self* although you can legitimately rate your acts, deeds, traits and performances. Remember that you are always a *person* who at times behaves well or badly but is never a *good person* or a *bad person*. No matter how badly you may have fallen back and brought on an old disturbance you thought you had got rid of for good, you can still accept yourself with your weak or foolish behaviour.

Once you can accept yourself as a person who, on this occasion, has once more acted badly, but is not a bad or inadequate person, you can then tackle your problem of anger as you successfully did in the past. In other words, use the A-B-C framework to guide you and remind you of how you identified and tackled your iBs and self-defeating behaviours previously and how you can continue to use these insights now and in the future. Then when an old, or even a new, emotional problem such as anger or shame or anxiety arises to trouble you, the framework will provide you with your bearings and help you to plot a course leading to a rational interpretation and successful resolution of the problem.

2. Remind yourself of the three major iBs we drew to your attention many times throughout this book. Let's just list them here once more:

Major irrational Belief No. 1

'Because it would be highly preferable if I were outstandingly competent and/or loved, I absolutely should and must be; it's awful when I am not, and therefore I am a worthless individual.'

contd/...

Major irrational Belief No. 2

'Because it is highly desirable that others treat me considerately and fairly, they absolutely should and must, and they are rotten people who deserve to be utterly damned when they do not.'

Major irrational Belief No. 3

'Because it is preferable that I experience pleasure rather than pain, the world absolutely should arrange this and life is horrible, and I can't bear it when the world doesn't.'

Keep forcefully and persistently disputing these iBs whenever you see that you are letting them creep back again. Even when you are aware that you don't actively hold these iBs, realise that they are practically never entirely gone from your thinking patterns. They may not be troubling you right now but that doesn't mean they are dead. They may arise once more, so bring them to your consciousness and *preventively* and vigorously dispute them.

3. Keep risking and doing things that you irrationally fear, such as taking decisions which carry no guarantee of working out as you hope. Once you have done all the necessary background and preparatory work and the time has come to act, then act. If you feel uncomfortable about taking certain kinds of decision even when you know they are the right decisions to take, don't allow yourself to avoid taking them – and thereby preserving your discomfort forever! It is often a good idea to make yourself as uncomfortable as you can be, in order to eradicate your irrational fears and to become unanxious and comfortable later.

4. Try to see clearly the difference between appropriate negative

feelings – such as those of sorrow, regret and disappointment when you are frustrated and do not get some of the important things you want- and inappropriate negative feelings – such as those of depression, anxiety, self-hatred, self-pity or anger when you are deprived of desirable goals and plagued with undesirable things. Whenever you feel an inappropriate negative feeling like being over-concerned (panicked) or unduly miserable or depressed about some event or possible happening, you are bringing on these unhealthy feelings by believing in some dogmatic *should, ought* or *must.* As we keep reminding our trainees and clients, 'cherchez le should!' These *musturbatory* beliefs are there, sure enough. Look for them, don't give up until you actually do find them and change your upset feelings by disputing the iBs which lie behind your upset feelings and replacing them with more rational desires and preferences.

Before you stop your disputing and before you are really satisfied with your rational answers to it, keep disputing until you are *fully* convinced of your rational answers and your upset feelings have truly disappeared. Do the same thing many, many times until your new rational philosophy becomes a part of you which it will if you keep working at it.

5. Remember – and use – the three main RET insights.

Insight No. 1

You mainly feel the way you think. When unpleasant events or frustrating circumstances happen to you at point A, you can select rBs that lead you to feel appropriately sad or regretful, or you can select iBs that lead you to feel anxious, depressed, angry or self-hating.

contd/...

Insight No. 2

Regardless of how you originally acquired your iBs and self-sabotaging habits, you still choose to believe and hold on to them today. That is why you are *now* disturbed. Your past history and your present life conditions affect you, but they don't *disturb* you. Your present philosophy is the main contributor to your *current* disturbance. In other words, if you are upset today, it is because you still actively hold on to early acquired views and refuse to re-think and act against the iBs which you originally upset yourself with. We all carry around a lot of baggage acquired from the past. If you find that some of it is holding you back from living a more satisfying life – dump it! In this book we have shown you how.

Insight No. 3

Merely changing your thinking is not in itself likely to be enough to enable you to bring about lasting personality change. Acquiring basic personality change requires persistent work and practice at disputing cognitively, emotionally and behaviourally, your iBs, and changing your inappropriate feelings and self-destructive behaviours for healthier and more productive feelings and behaviours.

---

6. Look for personal pleasures and enjoyments and other absorbing interests. Make one of your major life goals becoming a peak performer at work, but in addition try to become involved in other long-term interests in which you can remain truly absorbed. A good happy life is something to live for.

7. Avoid procrastination! Do unpleasant tasks fast – now! If you still procrastinate, reward yourself with things that you enjoy

after you have performed the tasks that you easily avoid. If that doesn't work, give yourself a severe penalty such as giving a large sum of money to a cause you detest. You will find that tackling the avoided task is not so bad by comparison.

8. Finally, look upon maintaining your emotional health and keeping yourself reasonably happy as something of a *personal* challenge no matter what misfortunes befall you. You are a human, not a defenceless laboratory rat or guinea pig. You *can* think for yourself. You almost always have some *choice* about how to think, feel and behave. You don't have to follow the dictates of your culture, or feel obliged to take seriously the fads and fancies of the moment. Every prejudice from whatever source it comes can be examined, scientifically questioned, evaluated and rejected.

Using the principles of Rational-Emotive Training, resolve to work and work at uprooting the sources of any emotional difficulties you may experience until they rarely trouble you. As with any other acquired skill, work and practice is necessary. It won't make you perfect, but it will propel you in the right direction!

The theme of this book has been achieving peak performance at work. As a person in a responsible position in your organisation you presumably are using your management skills and your uniquely human problem-solving abilities to chart and forge an upward path to the realisation of your corporate objectives and the achievement of your own personal goals. We hope that the principles of Rational-Emotive Training we have been teaching throughout this book will help you to reach your objectives by showing you how to overcome those all too human failings which can lower one's efficiency, slow down progress, or even bring it to a halt completely; failings like procrastination, performance anxiety or anger at colleagues whose own inadequacies may be blocking your advancement – all of these can pose problems which may temporarily, at least, derail your efforts to achieve peak performance.

At the same time, however, we are fairly sure that most of you reading this book will have realised that the Rational-Emotive Training you have been absorbing – and hopefully applying – in your work, can be employed equally effectively in other areas of your life. As we have argued in this final chapter, your work is an important, maybe the most important part of your life, but it isn't necessarily the whole of life. Some of you may choose to make it so, but no matter how absorbing and vital an interest your work may have become, you can still engage in other activities which could be nearly, if not quite, as absorbing as your work, and which could be enjoyable in their own right and very rewarding in terms of personal growth if you were to put the requisite effort into them. Peak performance, in other words, doesn't just apply to work! But if you conscientiously strive to apply the principles of Rational-Emotive Training to the whole of your life, and to organise it through devoting yourself to a few vital absorbing interests, we don't promise that your life will be a real ball; but you'll find our work and methods can be a great help towards it! We wish you success.

Summary

- *We defined what we mean by the term 'workaholic' by listing a number of behaviours regarded as typical of workaholics. The main characteristic of workaholics was identified as a compulsive addiction to work. By contrast, the individual who loved to work and was dedicated, but not compulsively driven to work was termed a 'workaphile'.*

- *For clarity we indicated that we would denote compulsive workaholics by the single word, 'workaholic' throughout the text to facilitate our study of workaholism and the ways in which it differed from the attitudes to work of workaphiles.*

- *We identified the iBs which drove people into workaholism and contrasted these iBs with the rBs of the workaphile. We showed that the Beliefs of workaphiles consisted of preferences for meaningful and challenging work while the Beliefs of workaholics consisted of rigid demands and 'all-or-nothing' types of thinking.*

- *We then considered some possible disadvantages of workaphilism and suggested ways of alleviating or overcoming them.*

- *Next, we took up the question of how one could change from being a workaholic to become a workaphile. We outlined a number of cognitive, emotive and behavioural methods an individual could employ to weaken his or her workaholism and gave a number of examples of how these methods could be used.*

- *After emphasising the importance of maintaining a sensible health regime for anyone wishing to adopt a workaphile philosophy, we went on to suggest that the best way to maintain one's training gains would be to become a workaphile at Rational-Emotive Training.*

- *We continued on this theme by reviewing the salient aspects of the training including the three main iBs and the three RET insights. We emphasised the importance of work and practice at disputing common iBs and the desirability of reinforcing these cognitive methods of combating iBs with emotive and behavioural methods.*

- *We concluded by pointing out that RET principles could be effectively applied to areas of life other than that of work. We suggested that by aiming for peak performance in whatever activities you wished to select in life, in addition to the area of work, you could significantly enhance your chances of living a happy and fulfilling life.*

References

Buzan, T., *Make the most of your mind*, London: Pan Books, 1988.

Cayer, M., DiMattia, and Wingrove, 'Conquering evaluation fear', *Personnel Administrator*, 33(6), 1983.

DiMattia, D., 'Using RET effectively in the workplace'. In M. Bernard (Ed.), *Using RET Effectively*, New York: Plenum, 1991.

DiMattia, D.J., with Mennen, S, *Rational effectiveness training: Increasing productivity at work*, New York: Institute for Rational-Emotive Therapy, 1990.

DiMattia, D.J. et al, *Mind over myths: Handling difficult situations in the workplace* (cassette recording), New York: Institute for Rational Emotive Therapy, 1987.

DiMattia, D.J., and Long, S., *Self directed sales success* (cassette recording), New York: Rational Effectiveness Training Systems, 1990.

Ellis, A., *Executive Leadership: The rational-emotive approach*, New York: Institute for Rational Emotive Therapy, 1972.

Ellis, A., 'A rational-emotive approach to acceptance and its relationship to Employee Assistance programs'. in S.H. Klarreich, J.L. Francek, and C.E. Moore (Eds.), *The human resources management handbook* (pp. 325-330). New York: Prager, 1985.

References

Ellis, A., and Blum, M., 'Rational training: A new method of facilitating management and labor relations'. *Psychological Reports,* *28*, 1267-1284. Reprinted: New York: Institute for Rational Emotive Therapy, 1967.

Ellis, A., *Anger: How to live with and without it,* Secaucus, N.J: Citadel Press, 1977.

Ellis, A., 'Research data that support RET clinical and personality hypotheses', in A. Ellis and J.M. Whitely (Eds), *Theoretical and empirical foundations of rational-emotive therapy,* Monterey, CA: Brooks/Cole, 1979.

Ellis, A., and DiMattia, D. *Rational effectiveness training: A new method of facilitating management and labor relations,* (rev. ed.) New York: Institute for Rational Emotive Therapy, 1991.

Ellis, A., 'The untired rational-emotive therapist', *Voices,* 15(2), 34-35, 1979.

Ellis, A., 'The value of efficiency in psychotherapy', *Psychotherapy,* 17, 414-419, 1980. Reprinted in Ellis, A. and Dryden, W. *The Essential Albert Ellis.* (pp. 237-247). New York: Springer, 1990.

Ellis, A., 'My philosophy of work and love', *Psychotherapy in Private Practice,* 1(1), 43-49, 1983.

Ellis, A., and Knaus, W., *Overcoming procrastination,* New York: New American Library, 1977.

Kirby, P. and DiMattia, D., 'A rational approach to emotional management', *Training and Development Journal,* 45(1), 1991.

Klarreich, S.H., 'Stress: An interpersonal approach'. In S.H. Klarreich, J.L. Francer, and C.E. Moore (Eds.), *The human resource handbook* (pp. 304-318). New York: Praeger, 1985.

Klarreich, S.H., 'Stress is in the eyes of the beholder', Exxon, Manhattan, April 23, 2-3, 1982.

Klarreich, S.H., *Work without stress,* New York: Brunner/Maxel, 1990.

Lyons, L.C., and Woods, P.J., 'The efficacy of rational-emotive therapy: A quantitative review of the outcome research'. *Clinical Psychology Review*, 11, 357-368, 1991.

Miller, T. (Speaker), *Self discipline and emotional control*, Video cassette, Boulder, CO: Career Track, 1992.

Siegelman, E. Y., *Personal risk: Mastering change in love and work*, London: Harper and Row, 1983.

Viscott, D., *Risking*, New York: Pocket Books, 1979.

Von Oech, R., *A whack on the side of the head*, London: Thorsons, 1990.

Index

Index